How to Have Fun with Kids
& Grandkids Using Video Chat

How to Have Fun with Kids &
Grandkids Using Video Chat

A Guide to Building Close Family Bonds with Chat Apps,
Skype, FaceTime, Google Duo, and Facebook

Website: http://www.videocallwithkids.com
Blog: www.videocallwithkids.com/connect

© 2020 Lillian Tibbles

Platinum Coast Press

Publisher's Cataloguing-in-Publication

Book cover Design by Travis Miles

ISBN:
978-0-9898818-3-8 (print)
978-0-9898818-4-5 (ePub)
978-0-9898818-5-2 (Kindle mobi)

Library of Congress Control Number: 2020906293

How to Have Fun with Kids & Grandkids Using Video Chat

A Guide to Building Close Family Bonds with Chat
Apps: Skype, FaceTime, Google Duo & Facebook

Lillian Tibbles, PhD

Platinum Coast Press

To my grandchildren Brandt, Elly and Joseph. Thank you for all the delightful video chats that you shared with me. And, to my husband Ken and my two children Lynn & Chris

Contents

Why I Wrote This Book

The video calls that I have shared with my children and grand-children have been a joyful part of my life for the past nine years. Since 2013, when I wrote my first book about this topic, the op-tions for making video calls, the parenting issues, and the online safety issues have changed greatly. This book updates that infor-mation.

Video calling, video chatting, and video conferencing all de-scribe an audio call that includes visual, face-to-face communica-tion using an application (app) like Skype or FaceTime, and an Internet connection.

When inviting family to video chat, I often say, "Do you want to Skype?" Friends who use FaceTime might say "Do you want to FaceTime?" All these terms refer to making a video call.

What most surprises me is that when I talk with parents and grandparents many are puzzled to hear they can do so much more during a video call than just talk with children. Research is telling us that we can and should do more if we want to develop close bonds and strong family relationships.

Today's families are often separated, and interpersonal relation-ships are conducted in a digital world. Our children and grand-children are connecting online with their friends. Parents and grandparents can also use this tool to connect with the children they love.

This book includes the best of each of my previous books and it shares the latest updates and research about children and video chat.

I have some very good news. We now know that video calls can be a powerful tool in building family relationships. Video calls can also be an effective tool for teaching and learning.

The *Connecting Generations* study released by the American Association of Retired People (AARP) and Microsoft shows that today's social technology helps families connect and improve intergenerational relationships. Video chat can help you stay connected with those you love when you are separated by just a few miles or by thousands of miles.

If you are looking for fun activities and suggestions for great video calls to your children or grandchildren, this book is for you.

My first grandchild was born when my daughter lived in Wyoming, over three thousand miles away from my home in Florida. Frequent travel of that distance was unlikely. Skype brought us into each other's homes and provided a simple and fun way to connect. For the past nine years video chat, our fun virtual visits, have allowed my grandchildren and me to build close relationships and we relish our time together.

Each week I put aside time to enjoy chatting while I share the excitement of watching my precious grandchildren grow and change. I was able to enjoy first smiles and first attempts at sitting, crawling, and walking during video chats. As babies it wasn't long before our grandchildren recognized their grandparents' voices and then our faces.

When my third grandchild arrived—also residing in another state, I was excited to see and hear him with video chat.

"Call Grammy and Grampy so I can show them," is a frequent request to their parents. Now, envision how excited children can be to tell you, and with video chat to show you, Halloween costumes, lost teeth, good report cards or even a cheerleading outfit or prom dress.

From infancy through the college years, seeing and talking to children with video call apps is far more fun than a telephone call.

Children need the care and love of the adults in their lives even when they are miles away. Although nothing is better than visiting those you love in person, video chat is a close second.

Whether you are a grandparent, divorced parent, a working parent who travels, or away in the military this book provides ideas to help you enjoy video chats.

Helping families build close bonds, stay connected, and stay safe online is why I wrote this book.

A Note from the Author

Writing a book for adults about how to use any technology can be a challenge.

Tech savvy adults who have used computers for years need little guidance to navigate the apps available for video chat.

Others who pick up this book will have less experience or only basic information about surfing the web and using the apps on their phones, tablets, and personal computers.

Those who are familiar with technical terms, software, and hardware can start right in with Part I, the information about what children enjoy at different ages.

I have tried to keep it simple for those new to using the Internet or video chat. Browsing through the section on Technical Terms will be helpful before you begin Part I. I encourage you to return to those definitions if you come across a term with which you are unfamiliar.

Most of all, at all levels of comfort with technology, be sure to read Part I to learn what children enjoy at each age. That information is important to make your calls fun for both you and the child you are calling.

Lastly, but very important, if you have purchased this book as a parent or grandparent, consider giving a copy to the parent with whom the child resides. That way you will have the same knowledge and understanding about what works well when video chatting with children.

Part I

Video Call: A Fun Communication Tool

1.

A Tool for Building
Relationships & Close Bonds

In 2011 the American Academy of Pediatrics (AAP) warned against screen time for children under the age of two because of potential risks and the lack of research about benefits. In 2016 when the AAP Guidelines were updated, they specifically stated that video chat was not included in the screen time restriction.

What has changed? We now know that video chats can be both a strong communication tool and an effective educational tool. Video calls allow for interactions between the caller and the child that other forms of screen time do not.

We also know that video calls can help you and a child build a close relationship and social bond.

Many parents and many more grandparents are separated from the children in their families. Video chat is a tool that you can use to bring those children closer. Building a close bond and a long-term relationship with a child will be your reward.

How do you go about building strong bonds? It's very simple, the child needs your time and attention. Video call makes this possible even from a distance.

Scientists studying video chat with babies and young children have found that the gestures and affection seen during a video call are enjoyed by the child and can also help them to learn. Unlike a television cartoon or a prerecorded video, a child understands that a video chat is real.

More evidence continues to show us that young children not only learn better using video chat than other forms of screen time, but also recognize and prefer a video chat partner over a teacher who was prerecorded.

Parents and grandparents can use video calls to provide unconditional love and to provide a safe harbor for children to discuss fears and share accomplishments.

Even adults who are far away from a child have an amazing opportunity to help that child explore problems, find solutions, and manage frustrations all while making a video call.

Calls to school-age children can encourage positive actions and develop a child's sense of self-esteem. Video chat is a personal and special way to connect with a child.

Child development expert Dorothy Einon reminds us to keep the scales of praise and criticism weighed in the direction of praise. This is good advice for video calls. Connect by listening and looking for opportunities to use praise and applaud efforts.

2.

Having Fun with Your Children & Grandchildren

Knowing some basic information about what children can do and what they enjoy doing at different ages and stages of development is important for bonding. It helps parents and grandparents know what a child will be able to respond to, whether you are with the child or using a video call. That knowledge will make video calls more fun for both adults and children.

No two children develop in the same way. Keep in mind that the descriptions presented here are very general. Some children will master skills earlier and others later.

In *The Essential First Year*, Penelope Leach describes milestones like rolling over, sitting, crawling, and standing as useful reminders of *what* we can expect from babies. But she also reminds us that they tell us little about exactly *when* we can expect those skills.

Adults can encourage development through play. Children love repetition. Older children often find pleasure in activities that they enjoyed at a much younger age.

Simple games like peek-a-boo can teach important concepts. This favorite game teaches object permanence, helping the baby to understand objects exist even when they cannot be seen, heard, or touched.

Jill Stamm, co-founder of New Directions Institute for Brain Development, has explored how children's brains develop. In her book *Bright from the Start*, she talks about the importance of repetition for learning and the role repetition plays in making strong connections in the brain.

Repeating favorite songs, games, jokes and riddles, and reading favorite books many times can make your visit with video chat both comfortable and fun. My grandchildren often ask to see the same hand puppets and books from one call to another.

Attention span is another important consideration when interacting with babies and toddlers. Attention span, the length of time during which a child can remain interested, is very short. It can vary with the temperament of each child and their age. Babies may be interested in a song or game for just a few seconds, toddlers for a few minutes.

In addition, the type of activity and whether a baby or toddler is hungry or tired will also influence their attention span. Best to let babies and toddlers rest when you begin to lose their attention.

In fact, parents or grandparents can influence the amount of time a child stays focused. Positive responsiveness in your facial expressions as well as praise have been shown to extend attention.

Whereas, interfering or preventing a toddler from directing their own play may cause frustration and shorten attention span. If a child is already involved in play or a task when you call, be an observer for a few minutes rather than disrupt what they are focused on.

Two children the same age playing together often have different skills. It is important not to compare your child or grandchild with other children the same age. Parents should seek advice from the child's health care provider if they have questions or concerns about development.

After reviewing the chapters about ages and stages of development, you may want to explore additional resources. Books such as The American Academy of Pediatrics Guide *Caring for Your Baby and Young Child* is an excellent resource. On the Internet visit the Centers for Disease Control and Prevention (CDC), which has a very helpful website:

https://www.cdc.gov/ncbddd/childdevelopment

Other websites where you can learn more about child development include:

www.babycenter.com

www.scholastic.com

www.pbs.org/parents

Tips for Fun Video Chats

You will quickly learn what kind of video calls work best for you, the child, and the child's family. Take the following into consideration:

- Young children's attention spans are short so keep the call length short.

- Not all babies and children enjoy the same activities or enjoy them at the same age, experiment with different activities.

- When children are tired, hungry, or frustrated about something, don't expect them to enjoy chatting especially between the ages of two and three.

- As you use this book to find age appropriate activities, consider activities listed for ages younger and sometimes older than the child you will be calling.

- Once a child moves from one age to another, don't hesitate to go back to activities listed for younger children. Children love repetition and returning to favorite games and songs.

- Engage young children by using props such as finger or hand puppets, and stuffed animals or by playing games like peek-a-boo.

- Talk with the child's parents about the length of call that is comfortable for the parent and the child. Call at their convenience and don't overstay your visit.

3.

Connecting with
Infants and Babies

Begin your relationship with an infant by connecting with sound. Baby's distance vision is limited and will take several months to develop. However, a newborn's sense of hearing is well developed. Baby has been listening to sounds inside the womb for many months. Parent's voices are recognized, as are the voices of others who were frequently with the pregnant mother.

In the Yale *Child Study Center's Guide to Understanding Your Child*, the authors tell us how important sound is to babies. After birth, a baby is more likely to recognize his father's voice if the father talked to the baby while it was still in the womb!

Parents, grandparents, aunts, uncles, and siblings can begin a relationship with video chat so the baby will recognize their voices, even if they are not with the baby frequently.

Playing the echo game by repeating the sounds that a baby makes is an interactive activity you can begin at a very young age. Another fun, interactive activity is to have the person caring for the baby play pat-a-cake while the caller sings the song.

Babies don't see as well as older children, but a bold black and white pattern may draw their attention. Vision improves during the first few months and color vision begins to come into place in just weeks.

Especially enjoyable is seeing baby's early movements as baby begins to stretch arms and legs. Some motions are mainly the result of reflexes or automatic responses such as sucking or closing the eyes to bright light.

Movement will be jerky; hands are usually clenched; baby can't control hands but may begin to watch them. Baby's sight is not clear; seeing only a short distance and will not see you on the computer monitor for a while. For the parent or grandparent who is miles away, seeing the newborn baby is a wondrous experience.

Enjoying a video call with babies takes a little planning. New parents are excited to share the joy of the new addition, but they are often tired. In our family we usually decide in advance the time that is best for us to make a video call.

Just prior to calling check to be sure the time is convenient for all. My children often initiate the call by texting me when the time is best for my call.

Be flexible when change is needed in arranging calls and keep the calls short for babies, toddlers, and tired parents.

Activities Babies Enjoy During
the First Two Months

- Connecting to the sound of your voice—use high tones and a gentle sound.

- Hearing the sound of a rattle or the ringing of a bell.

- Listening to you sing a favorite children's song, such as Twinkle, Twinkle Little Star, Row, Row, Row Your Boat, or The Farmer in the Dell.

- Hearing you play a musical instrument.

- Playing the echo game by repeating baby's sounds—watch for smiles.

- Following moving objects, especially toys and mobiles with strong geometric shapes.

Baby's skin is sensitive; the person who is with the baby can hold and stroke the baby during the video call, so the baby connects a loving touch with the sound of the voice.

4.

Fun for Months
Three & Four

Baby's distance vision is improving. Bold black and white patterns are enjoyed. Color vision is in place by 4-5 months. Bold colors like red, green, blue, and yellow can be seen.

Baby will be able to see you on the computer screen. She may even notice her own picture on the screen during a video chat with the picture-in-picture feature of the apps. At this stage babies sometimes smile at their own picture on the computer as they might do in a mirror.

Some control over hands, arms, and legs is beginning during these months. Smiling to get your attention is one of baby's newest tricks. Smiling may be followed by some babbling to really engage you. Responding to baby's sounds lets her know that she is important to you.

Games with touch or sound increase the interaction. For example, as the caller pretends to blow air toward the screen the parent can tickle the baby's face by gently blowing at it. Reading and singing songs can also be interactive as children grow.

A supportive seat on Mom's lap is a good spot from which baby can see the computer screen as she still can't hold her head up for long periods at this age. A baby seat, bumpo, car seat, or activity center are all ways to change baby's position for viewing the computer screen.

Placing a laptop or tablet on a sofa seat or low table and the baby on the floor can bring the webcam low for a better view.

If baby is restless parents can change baby's position several times during a video call to keep baby's attention and to provide an opportunity for the viewer to see what baby can do. She may look sideways while on her back or pick her head up while on her tummy. One of my grandchildren loved being in a baby jumper and we all giggled along with her while we enjoyed watching her bounce in the jumper during a video call.

Activities Enjoyed at Three
& Four Months

- Seeing bold patterns and primary colors. A bright toy or board book will direct baby's attention to the screen.

- Playing interactive games with touch and sound. Games are fun for you and delight baby. Some favorites are Itsy Bitsy Spider and pat-a-cake. With Itsy Bitsy Spider the parent can play the game by moving his or her fingers up baby's arm while you sing the song. With pat-a-cake, you can sing the song while the parent pats baby's hands together.

- Watching a short puppet show. Small finger puppets in bright colors are intriguing to babies. A small red lobster finger puppet that we named Red has been a favorite of our grandchildren.

- Listening to stories. Don't forget baby's short attention span; select a short book with bright pictures and few words. Hold the page close to the webcam so it can be seen. Books with sounds can also be fun.

Don't forget the importance of interacting when baby attempts to engage you.

5.

The Fifth, Sixth & Seventh Months

Fine motor skills are developing at this stage and the sound of a banging noise is an incentive for baby to use his hands. Physical coordination is improving. You may be able to see baby discover and grab feet and toes and put them in his mouth.

Baby's hand control is improving, and he may reach out for an object and bring it to his mouth. When making a video call try this interactive fun. The parent can help baby learn that he has two hands to have fun with by transferring objects from one hand to the other. The parent places a small rattle or other toy where the baby can reach it. Then helps baby transfer the toy to the other hand and back to the first hand. While observing during a video call you can clap and cheer as baby transfers the toy.

In the second half of the first year, several new motor skills are attempted and mastered, such as rolling over, sitting, crawling, and standing. Baby may roll from his back to his tummy and from tummy to back. As baby's ability to sit comfortably improves it will create a shift in how he views the computer screen. Remember that there is wide variation in the age when these motor skills may first appear.

At this stage baby can recognize his name, say "Mama" and "Dada" and may put two to three words together. He may feed himself crackers, hold a cup with two hands, and drink with assistance.

By the sixth month, vision is well established, and baby may enjoy seeing himself in a mirror or on the computer screen. At this stage baby will start learning to interact with you. Babies want to participate and get your attention. They may clap their hands, wave hello and goodbye, and blow kisses. By this age, simple games are fun.

Activities Enjoyed at Five, Six and Seven Months

• Playing peek-a-boo using a scarf, towel, hand puppet, or just your hands. If you say peek or boo with enthusiasm and a smile, you will likely get a delightful reaction. Vision is improving so enthusiasm and facial gestures go a long way to delight babies.

• Playing This Little Piggy. The baby sits on the parent's lap facing the web camera. The parent touches or wiggles the baby's large toe while you say or sing *this little piggy went to market.* At the next toe say *this little piggy stayed home,* then at the next toe *this little piggy had roast beef* (or substitute another food like carrots). Move on to the next toe with *this little piggy had none.* While the parent wiggles the small toe, you say—*and this little piggy went wee, wee, wee, all the way home.* Be creative, you can substitute activities or foods that the child enjoys in this game.

• Using simple words: hi, mama, dad, dog, cat, bird. Listen for babbling sounds in return.

• Asking questions: "Where is Mommy?" "Where is Rover (the dog)?" or "Where is Fluffy (the cat)?

• Using baby's name: "Joseph, would you like me to read a book?"

• Stacking blocks, and then knocking them down with a laugh—baby might surprise you with a laugh in return. Ask, "What happened to those blocks Elly?"

- Making sounds by banging toys like stacking cups, pots, and pans. Sit back and watch the fun when baby is given a surface to make noise on.

- Rolling balls are very tempting for baby to watch, push, or chase, especially if baby has begun to crawl.

- Continuing to sing songs and try the scales, Do, Re, Mi.

- Watching and encouraging baby to put objects in a shape sorter and poke at shapes with little fingers.

- Jumping in a baby jumper or bouncer can be great exercise for baby and continues to be fun for you to see during a video call.

6.

Watch Them Grow
Eight to Twelve Months

Now the fun really begins, baby is much more mobile. With video calls, you will see obvious and delightful developmental changes from week to week. Catch baby's first attempts to get to a sitting position and early attempts at crawling or creeping on hands and knees. You may see him reach out for toys he enjoys. With parents' permission, call at mealtime and watch him eat, or if he loves his bath, suggest a call at bath time.

Sitting without support may be possible but baby may topple over while you watch. Be careful not to appear upset as he will soon figure out how to get back to a sitting position.

In just a short time you will see your little one pulling up to stand and walk while holding on to furniture. How exciting to see him crawling toward the computer screen and standing up to see you better. My grandchildren loved waving hello or goodbye at this age. Try demonstrating a wave as you might be surprised to see it accomplished between months nine and twelve.

Finger foods are starting to be introduced. You can observe baby eating puffed and o shaped cereals. Small, soft pieces of fruit or cooked vegetables are enjoyed. You could demonstrate eating the same food during the video call and talk about how "yummy" the new food is.

Repeat simple words that baby knows, such as dad, mom, uh-oh, or bye-bye. Even if speech sounds more like gibberish at this stage, babies love to hear you repeat their sounds.

At twelve months babies may also attempt to repeat what you say and respond to your requests.

Activities Enjoyed from Eight to Twelve Months

- Repeating games baby enjoyed at a younger age, pat-a-cake and peek-a-boo with a scarf, towel, or your hands.

- Playing So Big—ask, "How big are you?" Parents can raise baby's arms up high while you say, "So big."

- Playing Where-Is by asking "Where is your doll?" or "Where is your truck?" Watch the child point, crawl, or walk toward the object.

- Drawing a simple picture with markers or crayons and proudly showing you his picture. The picture may only be a few lines, but he will be proud to show it.

- Listening to you read and viewing picture books.

- Watching hand or finger puppets. Start a puppet collection for video calls with baby as children enjoy them for many years to come.

- Making sounds. Boxes, bowls, and metal pans may be a little noisy but fun. Large spoons, paper tubes, egg cartons, and balls are all objects that children enjoy playing with and you can incorporate into a video call.

- Showing toy cars, trucks, airplanes, soft animals, or other toys that they enjoy sharing with you.

- Demonstrating their ability to walk and pull a toy. Favorite pull toys are often animals that make a sound, ducks that quack, and dogs that bark.

7.

Twelve Months
to Two Years

As children become more mobile, many more objects are of interest and reachable. Toddlers can hand objects to others as play. They will clap hands, say one word, and pull up to standing.

During this second year, toddling becomes a more mature form of walking. From thirteen to fourteen months, some toddlers will be able to walk well, pull a toy while walking, and pretend to be talking on a telephone. A few may be able to climb steps and match shapes.

By sixteen months, many will be able to stack three blocks, throw a ball, and run. A few will be able to kick a ball, brush their teeth, and say fifteen words or more. Watch their delight when they push buttons on toys that have parts that pop up.

Many enjoy demonstrating their skill in combing their hair or brushing their teeth. Our grandchildren enjoyed demonstrating these new skills during a video call. Send a new hairbrush, comb, or toothbrush for the demonstration. Opening the package and showing their skill will be a fun chat for the child.

With video call you can watch as the child holds a toy phone or pretends to cook, eat or drink. Simple games of pretend such as holding a doll or cuddling with a soft toy animal can be observed.

During this stage a toddler becomes more responsive. Language and comprehension skills are changing rapidly. By eighteen months some children can say "no" and say their own name. You can teach correct names and have him point to ears, eyes, nose, and mouth. Imitation is part of the learning process.

When our grandson visited at eighteen months, one of his favorite toys at Grammy's house was a jack-in-the-box. Sharing the toy again during a video call brought back delighted laughs and memories.

Blowing kisses toward the screen, which are then reciprocated by the viewer, is a favorite form of affection for toddlers and young children. Try ending your call with a bunch of kisses—my grandchildren love to blow kisses back to Grampy and me.

Activities Enjoyed from
Twelve Months to Two Years

- Showing off new skills like standing and walking. Send a pull-toy and watch the fun while the gift is opened, and the toy is pulled.

- Completing a wooden puzzle with large pieces that can be put in place while you watch.

- Stacking cups and blocks. Suggest that the child stack and knock down the blocks—you can demonstrate this skill on a table or the desk from where you are calling.

- Playing with toys with dials, buttons, and keys. These are great gifts and fun to watch the child play with during a call.

- Playing children's instruments, such as maracas, a xylophone, or a small drum. You might encourage a duet.

- Chasing or catching a medium size ball.

- Viewing picture books or magazines with bright pictures.

- Seeing a favorite toy that the child played with when visiting at grandparent's home can be fun for the child during a video chat.

- Pretending with a toy telephone.

- Demonstrating how hair is combed or teeth are brushed makes a toddler feel so grown up.

8.

Two to Three Years

The years from two to three are a time of rapid language growth. At two children understand most of what you say to them. Many twos have a good vocabulary and start forming sentences. The value of back-and-forth conversations is critical for language development. Communication during video chat provides this interaction, is fun, and easier to understand than a telephone conversation.

At two, many children know the names of familiar people, can follow simple instructions, and may repeat words overheard in others' conversations. They can identify pictures in a book such as a dog, baby, or cat.

Children at this age are mainly concerned about their own needs and desires. A two-year-old may display a broad range of emotions which you may see during a video chat as you would with any other face-to-face visit.

This stage is sometimes called the terrible twos and often extends through the threes. Temper tantrums can happen during video calls, especially if the child does not want to share his parent with you at the time of your call. If you see the child begin to get frustrated or restless, do something silly or distract him with a puppet or song that you can sing together.

One of my grandchildren's favorite puppets is a bear that disappears into a log. If he pops up in the corner of the screen when we are chatting with video it quickly gets their attention and brings a smile or giggle. It's a good distraction when emotions are high.

By keeping the video calls short and interesting you will be less likely to see frustration build and tantrums or meltdowns occur.

At times a child in this age group may decide that they don't want to participate in a video call at all. At these times it may be helpful to let him know, prior to a call, that Daddy or Grandma has a special book to read or instrument to play for him.

Don't forget that "no" is often a favorite word at this stage. There are times when our grandchildren did not want to participate in a video call. On those days, we just enjoyed chatting with our adult children and watching the grandchildren play with their toys. It didn't take long for the little one to come join the conversation.

Helping a two-year-old to identify their feelings or a three-year-old to recognize what causes their feelings is possible. When a child looks sad or frustrated you might ask how they feel or if they can tell you why they feel that way.

Children at two and three can also be very responsive and charming. They enjoy throwing you a kiss and hugging you (in person or symbolically during a video call).

As children move through the second year they begin to pretend to cook, eat, and take care of a baby. They start to name colors, sometimes correctly, other times incorrectly. You can play games that identify colors as the child gets closer to three years.

By age three many children will copy adult behaviors and those of their friends. They can separate easily from Mom and Dad and may continue chatting with you while a parent does household chores.

Three is a good time to give gifts of toys with buttons, levers, and moving parts. Pretend toys like toy household items, groceries, brooms, and tea sets are enjoyed. It's fun to watch them unwrap the gift and play with it.

After developing some steadiness in walking, children at this age enjoy ride-on toys that they can straddle and propel by their feet. At three years children begin to develop the skill of peddling and can enjoy a tricycle. They enjoy demonstrating these new skills during a video call.

By keeping video calls short and interesting you will be less likely to see frustration build and tantrums or meltdowns occur.

Activities Enjoyed at Ages
Two to Three Years

- Sharing their drawing, painting, coloring, or other artwork.

- Playing peek-a-boo continues to be great fun.

- Reading books with sound or listening to the reader make the sound (animals, trucks, or characters) while reading.

- Sharing an alphabet picture book.

- Building a tower and then knocking it down during the video call.

- Imaginative play with old clothes, dolls, play tools, pots, pans, and other props.

- Learning to sing some new songs, for example, *I'm a Little Tea Pot, Jack Be Nimble, Humpty Dumpty*, and the *Alphabet Song*.

- Surprising family member with a call to say or sing "Happy Birthday." With a little preparation from a parent, there will be excitement when special wishes are shared.

- Identifying colors of objects and toys.

- Playing hide-and-seek using a mobile device (smart phone or tablet) either indoors or out.

- Playing outdoors and sharing activities such as watering plants, playing in a sandbox, splashing in a pool, and riding a small toy with wheels or a tricycle.

9.

Four to Five Years

Video chats become very interactive during the years between four and five. Children will initiate conversations and enjoy sharing personal experiences with you. They may know what causes their feelings and understand that others don't always react as they do.

Pretend play is creative and imaginative. Children are fascinated with models, action figures, and small model cars. They can play for long periods with models such as dinosaurs, action figures and dolls. They will enjoy showing these to you during a video call. They might combine building blocks such as Legos with dinosaurs and share stories about what they have constructed.

I keep a box of action figures to use to play with my grandchildren. During a video chat we might each display Superman, Spiderman, or Wonder Woman. My grandson's figure of the Hulk might want to say hello to my figure of Captain America.

We can play with the puppets that I have in my home. My puppets like to talk to the puppets that I have given to the grandchildren that are in their home. The cowboy especially likes to visit with the chef.

Hand and finger skills also improve and children at this stage like to build objects and want to share them with you.

Riding a bike (possibly a balance bike or one with training wheels), hopping, jumping rope, swimming, throwing and catching a ball are all possible as balance and coordination improve.

Language skills are progressing and vocabulary has expanded. Children often ask universal questions about the color of the sky, the sun and moon, black holes, death and dying, and how birds fly.

Don't hesitate to say that you don't know the answer but will find the answer. Then, discuss the topic during a future call. There are many websites as well as children's books that answer these universal questions. Check with parents for any controversial topics.

Children begin to memorize their favorite stories and pretend to read. By age five many can count to ten or higher and enjoy showing you their new skill. Some children can print letters and their name.

Arts and crafts activities are interactive and great fun for children at this age. Creating memories and interacting socially to bond with our children and grandchildren is possible when working with arts and crafts during a video call.

Consider sending craft supplies and demonstrating how to make paper hats, airplanes, and cupcake liner flowers. Parents can have supplies ready on the child's end of the call so they can make the craft after the demonstration. Let the child's imagination shine, their flower doesn't need to look like the one you demonstrated to have fun.

Holidays afford many opportunities for craft projects that children will enjoy. There are many online sites and books at your library where you can find suggestions for age appropriate crafts.

Activities Enjoyed at Four and Five Years

- Assembling building blocks or other construction toys.

- Sharing objects that relate to the child's interests, such as dinosaurs, pets, dolls, action figures, and puppets.

- Completing simple puzzles.

- Demonstrating new skills such as standing on one foot, hopping, skipping, and dancing.

- Naming colors, numbers, and letters.

- Riding a bicycle, jumping rope and swimming.

- Playing games such as rock-paper-scissors, Simon Says, and hangman.

- Making a paper hat or airplane after you demonstrate how to do this.

- Reading a book—both fiction and nonfiction books are well received.

- Imaginative play is detailed and fun, play along with the fantasy the child creates.

- Discussing common children's questions or questions about concerns or fears such as *"Why aren't there any more dinosaurs?"* *"Why is the sky blue?"* *"Why do people die?"*

- Discussing a magazine or newspaper article that you have sent to the child.

- Playing hide and seek with the help of an adult and using a mobile device such as a smart phone or tablet for the call.

- Demonstrating a simple art or craft project that can be completed during a call.

10.

Six to Twelve
The School Years

During the early school years, children continue to develop their motor skills and problem-solving abilities. They develop greater independence from parents, and they form friendships. Children learn how to handle their feelings and resolve conflicts during this period. The pressures of peer relationships, school responsibilities, and performance grading all come into play.

School age children think in more complex ways. They begin to ask challenging questions. They can be quite independent at times and very dependent at other times. They may doubt and criticize parents or grandparents. However, they still delight in showing you their new skills and talents.

Because a child's sense of security is reliant on secure relationships with caring adults, parents and grandparents can have a great influence when they connect and communicate with video call. Feeling understood and accepted helps the child feel safe and secure.

When communicating with school age children, talk to them in a mature manner as they will become insulted if they think you are treating them in a babyish way.

Children during these years want to feel that you are listening to them. If you are concerned about how to respond to requests or questions take time to think about your response. "Let me think about that," or "Will you tell me that again?" are better responses than a quick "yes" or "no."

Body image issues used to be of greatest concern during the teen years. Unfortunately, children as young as five and six have become increasingly conscious of how they look to others. They may be subject to abuse or bullying by classmates if they are viewed as different.

During video chats it is important to let school age children express their feelings even if you don't agree with the way they feel. Avoid telling them that they shouldn't feel the way they feel. Instead you might want to say, "I can see how upset (or angry or afraid) you are" or "Can you tell me what upset you?"

You will thoroughly enjoy chatting with your school age child or grandchild as their ability to communicate becomes increasingly mature and their interest in the world expands.

Activities School Age Children Will Enjoy

- Sharing jokes and riddles.—see Rob Elliott's *Laugh Out Loud* books for some good ideas.

- Using a coin to play heads or tails.

- Playing games such as odds and evens, rock-paper-scissors, hangman, and tic-tac-toe.

- Using maps to see the distance between where each of you lives, to plan trips and to identify where world events are occurring.

- Sharing objects found in nature such as birds' eggs, leaves, a snakeskin, shells, or flowers.

- Reading a chapter book during several video visits can be enjoyed as attention span is increasing.

- Sharing a collection that a parent or grandparent enjoys, asking questions about objects collected and the similarities and differences in the collection.

11.

Good Times with Teens

Growing up isn't easy. No longer a child, yet not an adult, many teens assume that parents and grandparents don't understand them—and sometimes we don't. It is not unusual for families to experience a "disconnect" with teens.

The teen years are a time of rapid growth and development. Hormones change as puberty begins and that stimulates the growth of pubic hair in both sexes and facial hair in boys. Girls will develop breasts and start menstruating. Teens can worry about these changes and how they are seen by others.

Young teens may show concern about their body image and clothes. Some may show a lack of confidence in themselves and experience moodiness.

Increased interest in and influence by their peers is common. Sadness or depression can occur. Teens are beginning to develop their own identity and opinions. They are becoming less dependent on their parents. Although they have a greater ability to sense right and wrong, they also feel pressure to please peers which can lead to risky behavior.

The search for independence is a normal part of development. Parents sometimes see this part of development as a rejection or lack of control. When "being right" is the main issue conflict can develop.

Supportive relationships are critical to help teens with new concerns and to promote their positive development.

The teen years are also a time of creative self-expression. Using video chat, you can encourage new creative outlets to share. Introducing pre-teens and teens to the visual arts, photography, film production, music, and writing can be an exciting way to connect.

Key Points to Consider When Video Chatting with Teens

- Try to spend more time listening rather than talking.

- Try to understand without confronting, even if you disagree.

- Keep your comments short and don't lecture.

- Ask questions to explore thoughts & behaviors before making assumptions.

- Be willing to praise rather than criticize.

Here are some web pages with other suggestions for communicating with teens:

http://understandingteenagers.com.au/blog/5-mistakes-adults-make-communicating-with-teenagers/

https://www.psychologytoday.com/blog/hope-relationships/201404/9-tips-communicating-your-teenage-son

http://www.cnn.com/2014/02/19/living/talking-to-teens-communication-parents

Activities to Share with Teens

- Reading and discussing books and movies appeals to some teens. Use the video group call feature so two or more teens, who live in different households, can meet to share their thoughts about a book.

- Check out Anita Silvey's book guide *500 Great Books for Teens*. Check with the experts at your local bookstore and library for book suggestions.

- Don't limit your book selections to books that you assume are for adults. A popular read for teens is *The Book Thief*, a book that many adults enjoy. *The Book Thief* has won numerous children's book awards including the School Library Journal Best Book of the Year, Publisher's Weekly Best Children's Book of the Year, and Book Sense Book of the Year Award for Children's Literature.

- Many teens are disconnected from nature. Send nature books as gifts—books about animals, birds, and plants. Create activities that can be shared such as bird watching or hobbies and collecting.

- Discuss the environment and how we protect it.

- Take teens on field trips outdoors when they visit with you and discuss during video chats.

- Make a quilt with the teen creating squares.

- Learning to knit or crochet is appealing to some teens and can be taught during video calls.

- Play online games together.

- Teach about investing by selecting a stock to watch—use money from a game like monopoly for investing.

- Send art supplies such as colored pencils, pastel sets, artist quality watercolor sets, acrylic paint sets, calligraphy sets, and enjoy and discuss the art creations.

- Give a digital camera and/or photo design software such as Adobe Photoshop.

- Let your teen know about local and national resources for learning about radio production, film making, audio production, writing, and publishing.

- Suggest a field trip related to topics discussed during video chats when the teen visits.

12.

The College Student

Using video chat is one of the best ways to stay connected to your college age children & grandchildren. Along with typical college supplies, today's students are bringing smart phones and computers that have video call apps like Skype and FaceTime installed.

Colleges are developing Virtual Advising Centers where the student can schedule virtual appointments with their assigned advisor using videocall.

My children attended college long before video call apps were available. They enjoyed chatting by telephone on their way to class or while walking back to their dorm or apartment after class. Now parents, grandparents, other family members, and friends have the option of both seeing as well as talking to students.

Some college age students may prefer telephone to video chat, but many parents and students enjoy seeing each other on video. This is especially true for younger siblings who long to see their older brother or sister.

Discuss with your child or grandchild what type of communication they prefer. Pamela Cytrynbaum a college teacher, Mom, and

writer for the *Psychology Today* blog suggests that you discuss how, when, and how often you and the student will communicate.

Discussing both the student's expectations and your expectations may help to prevent disappointment. This also gives a student the opportunity to learn to become independent. Cytrynbaum recommends:

- Call often but do not pester.
- Calls should be frequent and short rather than occasional and long.
- Frequent does not mean every day.

A good source of information about communicating with college students comes from two experts, Barbara K. Hofer, a psychology professor at Middlebury College and Abigail Sullivan Moore, a New York Times contributor. Their book *The iConnected*

Parent: Staying Close to Your Kids in College (and Beyond) while Letting Them Grow Up provides some good advice:

- Be a great listener. Be in the moment. Give your child space to think out loud and to come up with his own solutions to problems.
- Respond appropriately to venting. If your child is venting about their roommate, a professor, or the miserable food, don't assume that you need to jump in with solutions.
- Let students initiate the calls or at least most of them.

The authors concluded that students who reported their parents initiated most of the calls were the least happy with the communication.

Show and Tell is still a favorite activity for students as they go off to college. The dorm room, the crowd at the football game, and a new friend are all fun for parents and grandparents to see during a video chat.

Be prepared to share some of your own activities. Ask teenagers for their opinions. Focus on positive news that the student may have an interest in. Don't always focus on the student's academic performance.

Part II

Video Chat Activities Enjoyed at Many Ages

13.

Fun with Video Chat Activities

Learning and social interaction begin in infancy and are encouraged by play at different ages. In each stage of play children learn important skills such as socializing, interacting, communicating, and problem solving.

Many of my grandchildren's favorite video chat activities have been enjoyed with increasing sophistication each year as they grow and change. This section explores those activities that are fun at many different ages.

Show & Tell

Show and Tell is the practice of showing something like a favorite toy, photo, or hobby to an audience and telling about it. This activity provides opportunities for children to speak, listen, and observe. It helps develop communication and public speaking skills. From toddlers to college age students sharing experiences is one of their favorite video chat activities.

Our younger grandchildren often bring their favorite toys to the computer screen and enjoy our comments and questions.

Showing us toy cars, superheroes, soft animals, and naming them has been a highlight of many video chats

Occasionally, a child will project their feelings and thoughts onto a puppet or superhero. A child might feel safer and find it is easier to share a concern by having a toy express the thought or feeling.

Adults can stimulate both conversation and learning by asking questions such as: What color is that? How many can you count? What shape is that? What letter does that begin with? How does that make you feel? Children relish positive feedback like seeing our faces light up when they identify an object, color, or shape that they are learning. We applaud as our younger grandchildren name the fire truck, dump truck, and police car.

Children of all ages love showing their artistic creations from day care, school, or special art classes. Favorite books and new clothes can be shared during a video chat. If the child doesn't initiate this sharing ask to see their favorite toy, cherished stuffed animal, or recent art project.

Children often bring home a favor when they attend a birthday party and enjoy talking about the party and showing what they have received. Our grandson was delighted to show us a toy snake that he received as a party favor.

Parents and grandparents who are making a video call can share objects from activities they have participated in. After a walk on the beach I might share a special shell that I found. A leaf, a feather, or special rock are all of interest to young children.

With older children I might read a fortune from a fortune cookie and discuss it. Reading newspaper articles about attractions that the children visited while with me in Florida can be a big hit. For example, the Lego exhibit at the botanical gardens or the new lion cubs at the local zoo. Showing my school age grandchildren cartoons that I see in the newspaper can be fun. A Dennis the Menace cartoon was a favorite.

Show and Tell is a simple activity that works well with video chat and helps develop both listening and speaking skills.

Reading & Book Clubs

Parents or grandparents can turn any video call into story time even when they are far away from the child's home. Consider reading a bedtime story during a video chat. Share the book's pictures by holding the book page close to the computer's video camera.

When reading to a young child, be enthusiastic about the story and try using different voices for different characters or props to sustain interest.

Consider the child's attention span when you select a book to read. Get suggestions by age from your local librarian, bookstore, or one of the online bookstores. Browse Pam Allyn's *What to Read*

When for an extensive annotated list of more than three hundred book titles for children from birth to ten years.

Reading out loud will quickly attract the attention of younger children. You can make the sounds yourself or select books that have sounds.

Books with sound that young children will enjoy are *Polar Bear, Polar Bear* and *What Do You Hear?* by Bill Martin Jr, *Around the Farm* by Eric Carle, and *Noisy Trucks* by Roger Priddy. Books with sound have great appeal to children 16 months or older.

We know that reading to children can help them advance their reading skills. And reading during a video chat is also great fun for both the child and adult. Once a child learns to read, take turns with the child, each reading one page.

Asking questions about the story helps develop comprehension and thinking skills. Learning the sounds that letters make is important for developing skill in reading.

Demonstrating your enthusiasm for reading encourages the child to read and to love books. As a child begins showing readiness for reading, he may want to reciprocate by 'reading' to you during a video chat. Sometimes children enjoy retelling a favorite story by pretending that they are reading. I adore when my grandchildren do this as it tells me that they love books and want to become readers.

Much to my delight my young grandson imitated my actions when first reading to me on Skype. He held the book close to the computer camera so I could see the pictures from the book that he was reading. Then, I could also see his pleasure in this accomplishment.

When my granddaughter began to read, she asked her mother to give us a video call so she could show us her new reading skills. It was so exciting for her to demonstrate her ability to read and it created a precious memory for her grandfather and me.

With older children consider reading poems, stories in a series, or newspaper and magazine articles related to the child's interest.

Dressing Up

Young children love to pretend and dress up in adult clothes. Wearing costumes of favorite characters such as superheroes is also great fun. Sharing the pride in a Halloween costume, or for older children, a scout uniform, a band uniform, or a prom dress is a special experience that they can share with you during a video chat.

- Send old dresses, shirts, hats, shoes, and jewelry and watch the fun.

- Make or purchase capes and enjoy watching your superhero fly around the room.

- Ask your superheroes what secret powers they have.

- Recycle old costumes or visit party stores, resale shops, and discount stores to find inexpensive costumes that can be used for play. Online costume resources are also available.

- Older children and teens enjoy showing uniforms, sports equipment, and event clothes.

- Preteens and teens who are learning to sew can share what they have made during a video call

Cooking

Many famous cooks credit their parents or grandparents for inspiring them to cook. Those with restaurants often continue to cook family recipes in their restaurants and on their television shows.

With portable devices like tablets and laptop computers you can create opportunities to share recipes. Children can watch you cook or cook along with you. Cook or bake something that they can see and then send it to them. Some examples are:

- Herbed popcorn
- Granola bars
- Fruit breads
- Brownies
- Cookies

Take a cue from your favorite TV cooking star and organize ingredients before the video call so you can put the ingredients together in an efficient and timely manner.

Music

Enjoying music during a video call is a delightful way to interact with children. Music is appreciated across the ages from babies to adults. Singing quickly drew the attention of my grandson at five months of age. As I began singing, he looked directly at me on the computer screen and smiled while his mother put his hands together and clapped.

Enjoy watching babies and young children smile, sway, or bounce up and down when music is played. The rhythm of music is very entertaining for children and stimulates development. Repetition of favorite songs and games is fun for children.

Older children often enjoy songs from movies like The Bear Necessities—*Jungle Book*, When You Wish Upon a Star—*Pinocchio*, Be Our Guest—*Beauty and The Beast*, Hakuna Matata—*Lion King* and *Un Poco Loco*—Coco.

A two or three-year old can play simple instruments. A good quality child's xylophone, tambourine or drum is great fun for the child to play during a video call.

Older children who are taking music lessons can share a new song they have learned. If both you and the child play an instrument, play a song together during your video call. You may be miles apart, but you will enjoy this activity as if you were in the same room

My friend Heidy's children and her grandchildren enjoy playing music during a video call. They sing along and dance to the music. Consider having your grandchildren teach you a dance step, have a dance party, or sing karaoke. A cheerleader could demonstrate a cheer to their school song.

Many adult songs are also appealing to children: Home on the Range, You are My Sunshine, This Land is Your Land to name just a few.

I've included a list of children's songs that you can sing or play on an instrument. If you are not sure about the words you can find them, as well as other songs, on the Internet.

Favorite Children's Songs

If you can't remember the words to a song, type the title into your search engine. The words to all these songs are available on the Internet.

Alphabet Song   Mulberry Bush
Baa Baa Black Sheep   Old McDonald
Baby Bumble Bee   There Was an Old Lady Who
Bear Went Over the Mountain   Swallowed a Fly
Bingo   Pat-a-Cake, Pat-a-Cake

Happy and You Know It

Happy Birthday

Head and Shoulders

Hey Diddle Diddle

Hickory Dickory Dock

How Much Is That Doggie in the Window

Humpty Dumpty

Hush Little Baby

I'm a Little Tea Pot

Itsy Bitsy Spider

Jack and Jill

London Bridge

Ring Around the Rosy

Rock a bye Baby

Row, Row, Row Your Boat

Do, Re, Mi......

Six Little Ducks

Skip to My Lou

Ten Little Indians

The Ants Are Marching

The Farmer in the Dell

This Little Piggy

This Old Man

Wheels on the Bus

Whistle While You Work

Twinkle Twinkle Little Star

Hobbies & Collections

Children as well as adults enjoy hobbies, those activities or interests undertaken for pleasure or relaxation. Hobbies can help bring people together and develop bonds. In addition, hobbies have numerous benefits for children. They can help develop competence, nurture creativity, build social skills, reduce stress, and help children to learn patience and self-discipline.

Hobbies can help a child feel like an expert. They can teach reading skills, personal responsibility, organizational skills, and math skills.

Collecting favorite items is a hobby that may begin in childhood and is often enjoyed through adulthood. Imagine the fun you could have sharing a hobby with your child or grandchild using video chat.

Share these hobbies:

Photography	Crochet
Knitting	Calligraphy
Lego or block building	Magic
Quilting	Jewelry making
Sculpture with clay or	Online games such as card
Play-Doh	games & Scrabble
Drawing	Painting
Coloring	Scrapbooking
Bird watching	Nature walks
Stargazing	Sports
Puzzles	Reading
Cooking	Baking
Gardening	Dance
Yoga	Music
Puppets	Sports

Examples of items commonly collected are coins, stamps, postcards, comic books, matchbox cars, dinosaurs, and dolls.

You can foster enthusiasm during a video chat by asking about a hobby or collection. You can help seek out and locate items for the child's collection and add to collections with gifts.

My grandson, who likes learning about dinosaurs, has had a dinosaur collection since age two. He is enthusiastic about sharing what he has learned about dinosaurs. He especially enjoys showing callers his dinosaurs during a video chat. And, when he visits, we seek out dinosaur exhibits in my area.

One of his favorite books that I often read during video chats is about a dinosaur. For special occasions I will send a new book about dinosaurs. I send him newspaper articles about dinosaur discoveries, and we can chat about the article during a video call. You can share interest in a collection in many ways.

Opening Gifts

Have you ever sent a gift to a child and then wondered what he really thought about it? A telephone call or a note thanking you for a gift is very nice to receive. However, it is priceless to see children open a gift that they really enjoy receiving.

"Grammy, I love it!!!" This gift, a puzzle that we watched our three-year-old grandson open during a video chat was a big hit. Excitement could be seen in his broad smile as he jumped and clapped his hands.

The reaction to the gift was a real treat. We also watched our grandson put the puzzle together with a little help from his Dad. When he finished, he said "Can we do it again?" It was a special moment and memory that we would not have had without video chat.

Opening a gift during a video call also gives young children an opportunity to identify with the person who is giving the gift. With video you are right there in the room enjoying that time together.

The wrapping is often fascinating for young children. What fun children can have breaking the air bubbles on gifts wrapped with plastic bubble wrap or playing with the paper and ribbon.

Be prepared, as the reaction to your gift may not always be what you expect or hope for. I once sent pajamas that I thought my two-year-old grandson would love. What I learned was that the stickers on the package were much more interesting to him than the PJs. As a result of being able to observe his response, I added stickers to other packages that I mailed, and I didn't send clothes to my other grandchildren until they were older and could enjoy that gift. However, it wasn't long before dinosaur pajamas were a big hit.

Sharing Jokes & Riddles

The ability to use humor is an important social skill and tool that can be used lifelong. A sense of humor can brighten our day and make being together fun.

Developing a sense of humor begins at an early age and the child's developmental stage can determine what makes him laugh.

When using humor, it is important to teach children that humor should make others feel good, it should not be hurtful.

Making funny noises or playing peek-a-boo with a smile and excitement is fun and funny to toddlers. Preschoolers often enjoy bathroom humor and may test you with their use of a favorite word like "poop." You might respond by saying that they are being silly rather than scolding.

Preschoolers begin to understand and enjoy knock-knock and silly jokes:

> Knock, knock.
> Who's there?
> **Olive!**
> Olive who?
> **Olive you!**

Why does a flamingo lift one leg?

Because if he lifted both legs, he would fall over!

Why do birds fly south in the winter?

Because it's too far to walk!

What is a volcano?

A mountain with hiccups!

Also:

- Play Make-Me-laugh—taking turns using humor.

- Wear a silly hat when you initiate a video call.

- School age children start to understand language and can spot different meanings to words. Nonsense words can get big laughs. Examples of nonsense words: balderdash, bugaboo, gibberish, hogwash, and poppycock.

- If you need some ideas for knock-knock and other jokes see Rob Elliott's *Laugh Out Loud Jokes for Kids*. Elliot has written several joke books for children.

14.

Celebrate Birthdays & Holidays with Video Chat

Participating in birthday and holiday celebrations with video call is a special treat. Holidays and other special occasions can be sad when families are separated. Travel during holidays is expensive and often unpleasant. Video call can take you where you want to be.

Birthdays

Celebrating a birthday with a video chat to sing *Happy Birthday* is fun to do. Watch as candles are being blown out and gifts are opened. With computers, tablets, and phones you can join in by watching a family celebration or children's party.

Organize a virtual birthday party by coordinating with several family members or friends to video chat at the same time.

It's fine to celebrate birthdays with a child on a date other than the actual birthday. We often celebrate with a video call the day before the actual birthdate and we prefer that.

The day of a child's birthday is so filled with activities and dis-tractions that it may not be the best day for a chat. Our grandchildren are always thrilled to know that they can open our gift a day or two before their birthday—it is seen as a special treat.

Most important, as with all video chats, be flexible with the day and time you call to accommodate the child and the child's parents. It will make your call more welcome than a surprise call on a busy day.

Holidays

Sharing holiday traditions, activities, art, and music during a video chat is fun for children and adults. It can also be a comfort for parents and grandparents who are miles away at holiday time. When I wear a Santa hat or wave a flag when calling on a holiday the children are looking forward to what we might talk about. Chatting about the holiday and reading books related to the special day is both a treat and a learning experience for all of us.

Celebrating holidays can provide an opportunity to learn about history, encourage understanding of diverse cultures, honor people who have contributed to our country, and learn about the changing seasons.

There are many great books written about every holiday. I have suggested just a few for each holiday. Use your computer search engine, or the experts at your local library or bookstore to search for special occasion books at the child's level. To use your computer to search, type *children's books about......* and name the holiday. You will get many selections to choose from. Here are some suggestions for celebrating holidays.

New Year's Day

The start of a New Year is often a time of hope for the future. In the United States the holiday is officially celebrated on January 1st. However, this is not the beginning of the New Year for all cultures and religions so adjust the date for your family and teach about the dates and celebrations for other cultures. Children often enjoy celebrating the beginning of a new year with hats and noisemakers. You might wear a hat and make sounds with different noisemakers when you make a call on New Year's Day.

Martin Luther King Jr. Day

Discuss who Dr. King is and why his life is celebrated. Read parts of his famous 1963 "I Have a Dream" speech and discuss it. Read *Martin Luther King Jr. Day* by Trudi Strain Trueit (2006) or *I Have a Dream* by Dr. Martin Luther King Jr. (2012).

Valentine's Day

This holiday is a great time to express and talk about your love for the child. Send a Valentine or materials to make a Valentine during a video call. Read *A Crankenstein Valentine* by Samantha Berger (2015) or *The Story of Valentine's Day* by Nancy Skarmeas (1999).

Presidents' Birthdays

George Washington's birthday is celebrated on the third Monday in February. Many states celebrate the holiday as Presidents' Day to include all the presidents. Wear red, white, and blue or have a flag displayed in view. Read *President's Day* by David Marx (2002) or *President's Day* by Anne Rockwell (2005). Older children can identify a favorite president and discuss their selection.

Saint Patrick's Day

You don't have to be Irish to enjoy this holiday. Tell or read stories about St. Patrick, elves, fairies, or leprechauns. Talk about the shamrock and wear green. Read *Saint Patrick's Day* by Gail Gibbons (1995) or *The Night Before Saint Patrick's Day* by Natasha Wing (2009).

Easter

Watch the fun as children decorate and color Easter eggs. Or have children decorate eggs in advance, then show and tell about their eggs during a video call. You might show eggs that you decorated before the call. Parents can hide a few eggs and you can watch the child hunt for them, with the parent using a mobile device. If appropriate in your family, you may choose to talk about the religious meaning of Easter and why we celebrate the coming of spring.

Cinco de Mayo

A fun day to celebrate Mexican heritage, culture, and pride. In Mexico the May 5th holiday marks the defeat of the French in the battle of Puebla. In the United States it is an opportunity for children to learn about another culture and the American hero Cesar Chavez, a civil rights leader who founded the National Farm Workers Association. Discuss favorite Mexican food and play Mexican music. Read *Off We Go to Mexico* by Laure Krebs and Christopher Corr (2008) or *Harvesting Hope: The Story of Cesar Chavez* by Kathleen Krull (2003).

Memorial Day

Discuss the meaning of this holiday; when did it start? If the children have attended a local parade, they will be excited to tell you all about it. Read *Memorial Day Surprise* by Theresa Golding (2004) or *The Wall* by Eve Bunting (1992).

Fourth of July

Talk about celebrating the country's birthday and play or listen to patriotic music. You can display a flag in the room where you are sitting or wave a small flag when you connect your video call. Read *History for Kids: The Fourth of July for Kids* by Ian Fraser (2013).

Ramadan

During the ninth month of the Islamic calendar you might discuss this Muslim holiday, which includes a month of good deeds, charity, and new beginnings. You could discuss the practice of fasting and talk about the Eid-al-Fitr festival. You might read *Night of the Moon: A Muslim Holiday Story* by Hena Kahn (2008) or *Tell Me More About Ramadan by Bachar Karroom* (2018).

Halloween

It is great fun for children to dress up in a costume but even more fun for them to show their costume to family. Dress up in your own costume to delight your grandchildren of any age. Some children use Halloween as a time to discuss their fears. Read *The I'm Not Scared Book* by Todd Parr (2011).

Veterans Day

Discuss war and peace. Talk about the importance of honoring those who serve to keep us safe from harm. Parents who are away on active duty may be able to discuss their work. Grandparents who served in the military services can share their experiences, show pictures, and uniforms. Read *Veterans: Heroes in Our Neighborhood* by Valerie Pfundstein (2012) or *The Wall* by Eve Bunting (1992).

Thanksgiving

Adults and children both benefit from taking time to warmly and deeply express appreciation for kindness and benefits received. Thanksgiving is a special time to teach children the importance of thankfulness. Share with them what gratitude is and what you are thankful for. Discuss the first Thanksgiving and have children share art projects related to this holiday that they made in day care or school. Read *the Thankful Book* by Todd Parr (2012) or *Happy Thanksgiving Curious George* by H. A. Rey (2010).

Hanukkah

Span the miles with Hanukkah love during a video call. Share the lighting of the Menorah candles with family by lighting your own Menorah at the same time as those you are calling. Watch children spin the dreidel and sing songs. Share your latke recipe or prepare latkes during a video chat. Read *Celebrate: A Book of Jewish Holidays* by Judith Gross (2005), or *The Clever Dreidel's Chanukah Wishes* by Sarah Mazur (2015).

Christmas

Help decorate the Christmas tree by sending some of your own family ornaments to share. Watch as the tree is decorated, or stockings are hung. Show the children your own decorations and share family stories. Sing or play carols with the children. Read

Bear Stays Up for Christmas by Karina Wilson and Jane Chapman (2008) or *The Christmas Star* by Marcus Pfister (2004).

Kwanzaa

Discuss the meaning of the word Kwanza and the African culture. Don't miss the opportunity to teach about a holiday that celebrates family, friends, and community. Read *My First Kwanza* by Karen Katz (2003) or *Together for Kwanzaa* by Juwanda Ford (2010).

Consider visiting the website www.apples4theteacher.com, a fun and educational website, where you will find holiday activities and crafts for children. Another resource is Scholastic. Scholastic publishes a series of **Rookie Read-About Holidays** books with titles for more than fifteen different holidays. Explore some of these titles.

Part III

Helpful Tips for Parents & Grandparents

15.

Tools for Special Situations

How to Ask Questions That Get More Than a Yes or No Answer

The secret to great conversations with children and teens is to ask questions that will produce more than a yes or no answer.

Here are some examples:

Who made you smile today?

What did they do?

What do you like most about school right now?

I heard that you had a great day in school today—can you tell me about it?

Did you catch someone doing something funny today?

What do you like to do after school?

Who brought the best lunch today?

What did they bring for lunch?

What would you like to talk about?

Did anyone do something super for you today?

I heard that you had a rough day—can you tell me about it?

What challenged you?

What happened next?

And then what happened?

What do you think you should have done?

What will you do next time?

I see that you have a haircut, lost tooth… etc.—tell me about it?

I feel sad about that; how do you feel?

I feel happy about that; how do you feel?

How can I help you?

What is the best thing that happened today?

What is the worst thing that happened today?

If you could have a superpower what would it be?

If you could be any animal what would you be?

If you could meet any living person or someone who lived in the past who would it be and why?

For Parents Not in Residence

Many parents are not in residence with their children. Parents who are divorced, in the military, or travel frequently for work. Some of the activities suggested in this book require a certain toy or piece of equipment to make the call interactive, playful, and fun.

Consider giving an age appropriate toy or add to a collection, for example, stamps or coins. Watch the child open the gift during a video call and then, or in later video chats, interact with the child as he plays with the toy or talk about the collection.

With younger children blocks, stacking cups, puzzles, pull toys, books, puppets, and children's instruments are all useful gifts that can make a future video call interactive.

Collect books and toys to keep in your residence, in your barracks, or in a suitcase if you are a parent who travels. Puppets, action figures, and books can fit into tight spaces. Use these props to get the conversation started or to draw the child back to you if they become distracted.

If you travel tell the child where you have been and share anything of interest that you have done or collected while away. Collect objects such as postcards or magnets from your location and talk about them during a video call.

Tips for Divorced Families

Video calls have become an important part of the parenting plan when couples divorce. As marriages end, custody issues can become contentious. Research does show us that after divorce, children do best when they have contact with both parents.

Being able to see a parent or child when one parent has relocated to a different home or out of state can be reassuring for both the parent and child. Language in a parenting plan can allow for video communication at "reasonable times for a reasonable duration."

Visitation is rarely denied by the courts unless it would "seriously endanger" the child. Flexible plans are often best if parents can co-parent without anger. It's ideal when parents can focus on what is best for the child and agree to make that happen.

Many divorced individuals as well as their children feel isolated following divorce, video calls can provide a means for staying in touch and for healing.

Peter Favaro, in his book *Smart Parenting During and After Divorce*, discusses the importance of making sure children stay in touch with both parents. His tips on how to avoid conflict through good communication are very helpful, as are his suggestions for co-parenting at different developmental stages.

Divorce distress can vary with the age of the child, and it is impossible to predict specifically how divorce will affect each child. Babies can feel the tension and stress in the household but cannot understand it. They may become irritable and cling to one parent.

Toddlers and preschoolers may become dependent and revert to more infantile behavior. They may feel anxious about the future and have nightmares.

Many parents are not aware that children of divorce can experience feelings of self-blame, loss, confusion, and sadness. Children need to hear and see both parents, even when one parent has fewer parenting skills than the other. Video calls are a great way to connect when parents are separated from their children.

Visitation via video call is often legally called **Virtual Visitation or Electronic Visitation.** It is sometimes called **Internet Visitation.** In addition to video call these terms also can refer to texting, email communication, and instant messaging.

In 2004 Utah became the first state to pass legislation for virtual visitation for parents. Michael Gough, a computer security expert and advocate for automatic options for virtual visitation, was instrumental in getting legislation passed. As a divorced father he wanted to stay regularly involved and available to his daughter. This became a challenge when his wife relocated over 1,400 miles away.

Some parents and grandparents need legal assistance to ensure that they can stay in touch with their children or grandchildren. Prior to 2007 there was little case law regarding electronic visitation. In 2007 a law was added to the Florida statutes giving both parents the right to communicate with their children using electronic means.

There are currently electronic communication laws in several states and pre-draft bills in many other states. Virtual visitation is usually the request of the noncustodial parent. This type of visitation may also be available in states that don't have specific laws when family courts rule to extend visitation electronically.

Like any other visitation, advanced planning for video calls is important. Parents who are working cooperatively can set the timing and length of electronic communication. What is reasonable for one parent may not be reasonable for another.

Daily calls may not be possible when the child's schedule includes extracurricular and academic demands. Bedtime calls can also be a problem in some families as the routine to calm the child and to get ready for bed is disrupted.

Birthdays, holidays, and special occasions can become a contentious point when visitation is not planned prior to the call.

If difficulty arises while establishing a workable electronic visitation schedule, consult with a mediator, counselor, or your attorney to develop the schedule. Respectful communication with any of our new technology, whether it is mobile phones, texting, or video call, is crucial for the child's welfare.

The Australian Parenting Network site www.raisingchildren.net.au and the Parenting network site www.parents.com have helpful tips for parents experiencing divorce. Just type divorce in the search box when you get to those sites.

Tips for Divorced Families
Communicating with Video Call

• Discuss in advance how the family will use video call technology.

• Speak positively of the other parent when calling; avoid using criticism or barbs.

• Continue to encourage the behaviors and limits that both parents have agreed upon.

• Give the child praise for positive ways that they are coping with the situations.

• Keep grown-up problems for grown-ups, don't worry the child with problems parents must solve.

• Create an atmosphere where the child feels safe to discuss their thoughts and feelings.

• Don't make promises that you can't keep.

• Don't ask your child to keep secrets.

• Avoid asking questions about what the ex-partner is doing.

• Avoid questions about the ex-partner's spouse or partner.

• Don't ask the child to choose sides or which parent he likes better.

• Make attempts to keep in touch with extended family.

Latchkey Children

Children returning to empty homes with keys tied around their necks have been called latchkey kids since the 1800's. The main reason children are left home unsupervised is employment of their parents.

It is estimated that 75 percent of single parents whose youngest child is between six and thirteen are working outside the home. Many two parent families need the income of both working parents.

Each day thousands of children are home alone after school despite the efforts of community groups, churches, the YMCA, and the Boys and Girls clubs. Grandparents often live a distance from young families and cannot help with childcare.

When a child is home alone, seeing a parent or grandparent can make everyone feel more comfortable. The technology of video chat can provide this opportunity.

An after-school video chat with grandchildren can be a special time for grandparents to enjoy the excitement as children share news about their day or their concerns.

Not all grandparents can assist with homework, but some can, and many more can provide emotional support to a child who is home alone.

Thanks to video chat apps parents and grandparents can see and talk to children who are home alone.

If a child will be using the Internet without adult supervision, be sure that parental controls, the privacy settings, and contact lists are all well managed.

The Hospitalized Child

My own experience of being hospitalized as a young child made me think about what a wonderful tool video chat can be for a child and their family when a child is hospitalized.

At the time that I was hospitalized my mother worked full time and had three younger children to care for. There were times when I was lonely and frightened knowing that a quick lunchtime visit from my mother might be all that was possible for my family on any day.

The unfamiliar hospital environment and invasive tests and treatments can make a child feel anxious and fearful.

There are also times when siblings and other family members cannot visit in restricted areas within a hospital.

The isolation can be worse for families that live far from the hospital. Video chat can bridge the distance between home and hospital.

Hospitals across the country are experimenting with this technology and studying the benefits. Results reported from The University of California, Davis Children's Hospital's study of 488 hospitalized children point to positive outcomes in children who have access to video conferencing.

Families in the study used a program called Family-Link. This program was meant to increase the frequency and quality of communication between hospitalized children and their families and friends.

Children who had access to the video chat program had a greater reduction in overall stress during hospitalization when compared with the children who did not use video call.

More information is also emerging about how technology can facilitate social support for ill children and adolescents. Video chat can help connect children and adolescents who have chronic conditions like lung disease and cancer with peers experiencing the same stressors. Peer mentors can provide valuable informational and emotional support.

Video conferencing is also being used to help students keep up with their classmates when they are hospitalized and unable to attend school. Boston Children's Hospital helps to bring students back to their classrooms to see their peers and to keep up with learning.

If you have a child or grandchild who is isolated because of health issues you might explore the availability of video conferencing.

For Those with Hearing Loss

If you have difficulty hearing take advantage of the extraordinary technology of video chat. Using video, you will be able to communicate with your family far more comfortably and effectively than by telephone.

Attempting to talk to a young child on the telephone can sometimes be a frustrating experience when hearing is compromised. One reason is we miss all the visual cues that help us to understand speech. My friends who are grandparents find the face-to-face contact of a video chat makes hearing and understanding much easier.

Chatting with video allows the caller to see the visual information important for understanding speech such as mouth movements and lip reading. Helpful visual cues also include facial expressions, and body movements and hand gestures. Sign language is also possible.

Studies have demonstrated that the ability to understand speech in people with severe to profound hearing loss can be improved when individuals use visual information plus audio. Video chat apps versus an audio only telephone will improve the ability to understand communication. Enjoy seeing those wonderful smiles from grandchildren with a video chat.

Another benefit of apps like Skype is the ability to use captions. This is possible with Skype's free online translator. The Skype Translator can also translate many different languages. The

Translator is available on devices with Windows 7 and above, Android devices, Apple devices: Mac, OS X, iOS, and Linux. You can learn more about Skype Translator from Skype support, at: https://support.skype.com/en/faq/FA34542/how-do-i-set-up-and-use-skype-translator.

Headsets and assistive hearing technology can also be used to improve your video chat experience. There are headsets with speakers for one ear or both. You can select wireless or wired devices.

Assistive technology like hearing aids and digital wireless accessories can help those with severe, profound, or single sided hearing loss. Don't miss out on the fun of communicating with your children or grandchildren because of hearing loss, consider using video chat technology.

Dyslexia & Reading Buddies

Dyslexia, a specific learning disability, is quite common in children. When I wrote my second book the prevalence was estimated to be between 10-15 percent of children in the US. However, two Yale academic physicians, Drs. Sally and Bennett Shaywitz, cofounders of the Yale Center for Dyslexia and Creativity, have reported that the prevalence is one in five children, although many have not been diagnosed.

The Shaywitzes have been studying dyslexia since 1983 and have enrolled over 400 children in their study. They define dyslexia as an unexpected difficulty in reading in an individual who has the intelligence to be a much better reader.

The child with dyslexia may have difficulty in reading, spelling, and performing skills related to the use of printed language. It is thought that the trait for dyslexia is inherited and runs in families. It is neither low intelligence nor laziness. Children with dyslexia can learn to read and go on to have successful careers.

Children who have dyslexia benefit greatly by targeted educational support, assistive technology, and audiobooks. Now envision having a child with a parent or grandparent who is supportive. You can be that reading buddy who reads to the child and enjoys having the child read to you. Video chat is a technology that can facilitate your involvement. Being a reading buddy is a wonderful role for grandparents or for a parent who is not in residence.

To learn more about dyslexia, explore the Internet. Two sites I can recommend are:

https://dyslexia.yale.edu/

http://www.mayoclinic.org/diseases-conditions/dyslexia/basics/definition/con-20021904

Video Chat with Adult Children

The real surprise for me in making video calls to my grandchildren is that it affords me a great opportunity to visit with my adult children. Seeing their faces, their expressions, and their homes is comforting. It truly is better than a telephone call.

When my friend Susan's adult son moved to another state, he suggested video calls, but Susan was very reluctant. She thought she would be uncomfortable being "on camera." As time went by and her son was less able to come home to visit, she agreed to try a video call. Susan was so excited to tell me about the call. They had agreed in advance about the time of the call and she was prepared. She loved being able to see her son's smile.

Sunday evening dinner visits are now routine. Susan sometimes invites her other adult children and the family has "dinner together" via video.

Video Chat on the Go & Outdoors

With portable devices such as phones and tablets you can make a video call outdoors or on the go. Seeing outdoor activities such as riding a bicycle, playing in the snow, or watching a sports event are all possible with video calls. Keeping the phone or tablet stationary or moving the device slowly keeps the quality of the picture high.

Roger Ryan, a backpacker who was vacationing in Australia, Skyped with his parents in Ireland during a parachute jump. That was much more exciting than a telephone call!

I have used a tablet outdoors to show my grandchildren the growth of a pineapple top which we planted during their visit. The children also enjoy seeing our small Florida lizards that they are fascinated with when they visit.

A friend plays hide-and-seek with her granddaughter. The child hides either in her home or outdoors while her mom searches with a phone during a video chat. The child can hear the grandparent's voice while the search is on. Grandparents can participate by saying "Where is—*child's name*—I don't see her?" They may hear the child giggling. There is lots of excitement when little feet can be seen beneath a curtain or hiding behind a chair indoors or a tree outdoors.

Demonstrating new skills outdoors, such as hopping, jumping, or riding on a toy is exciting for the child and entertaining for adults to see. When children have learned a new skill or have progressed to a new level of accomplishment, encourage them to show you what they can do.

Recently my grandson made a Skype call to show us that he had learned to throw a football. He proudly held a bright new football and we watched as a very strong pass sailed across the screen. It was great fun for all!

Take a phone or tablet to different parts of the home to see something that has changed. My grandchildren were excited to show me their new bunkbeds. Some outdoor activities that are fun to see during a video chat can include:

- Throwing or kicking a ball
- Skipping
- Jumping rope
- Riding a skateboard
- Riding a bike or scooter
- Swimming
- Making a snowball, snow man, or snow angel

Parents are the best resource about what the child's current outdoor interests and activities are; ask them so you can chat about those interests.

When I learned that my granddaughter caught her first fish while fishing with her Dad, I asked her to tell me about it during our next video chat. She was excited to share that story.

Hands Free Video Chat

Although I enjoy using my tablet and smart phone, I prefer my desktop computer for playing with my grandchildren during a video chat. The desk gives me a surface on which to place toys, crafts, or collections. Other family members use a laptop computer placed on a desk or other surface, so their hands are free.

If you are using a tablet or phone to video chat try using a stand, mount, or holder to enjoy being hands-free.

When I shared with my friend Kathy that I play with my grandchildren on Skype she was amazed. Her video chats were mainly chatting on FaceTime with the phone in her hand. She was surprised to learn that innovative stands, can make video chat easier and more fun. The bonus was that her grandchildren's attention spans were extended with interactive activities and play.

If you haven't tried playing during your video chats think about the possibilities for puppet shows, showing pictures in a book that you are reading, and teaching a child to knit. There are two-in-one tablets, such as the Microsoft Surface Pro, that have the stand built in. Stands for your existing tablet or phone are also available in many sizes and in a variety of materials and prices.

Finding a stand that works for you is a snap. There are stands for uneven surfaces like beds and sofas. A bed tray, bed table, or tablet stand can be a great gift for a child or grandparent who is bedridden and enjoys video chatting.

You can find reviews and pictures of these products online to help you decide which is best for you. Stands, mounts, and holders vary greatly in price from $7.99 to over $300. If you want to look at a variety of stands and holders, search tablet stands, cell phone holders, or phone stands for bed, on Amazon or check your local Staples, Best Buy, or Target for options.

Enjoy your next video chat hands free and imagine the possibilities.

16.

What You Need to Make a Video Call

To make a video call you will need:

- a computer, tablet, or mobile phone that can connect to the Internet.
- a webcam (web camera).
- external or built-in speakers.
- broadband or Wi-Fi to connect to the Internet.
- a video call app like Skype, FaceTime, Google Duo, Hangouts, or Zoom.

Many computers and phones have video call apps installed and are equipped with a camera and speakers. You need only to set up the video call app with your chosen screen name or telephone number, and a password, you are then set to go.

Don't miss out on the fun of video chat because the process seems complicated. If you are new to using technology, don't hesitate to ask a friend, family member, or tech specialist to help you set up your computer or phone to video call. It takes only minutes.

All Apple devices come with the FaceTime app installed. Windows devices and Android devices have the Skype app installed.

When you don't have the app installed that you want to use, you can download it to your device.

I'm a visual learner, if you are as well you might consider going to **Skype.com** or **Apple.com**, or **YouTube.com**. Browse through their HELP information. You will find video tutorials from the manufacturers and helpful videos from enthusiastic users of the different video call apps.

Or, using your Internet search engine type "how to make a video call with" and add the name of the app you want to use.

Choosing A Video Call App

When deciding which app to use you must consider the manufacturer of the devices that you will use—computer, tablet. and phone. Discuss with family members which devices they will use for the calls. Users on both sides of the call must use the same app.

Here are just a few of the many video call apps:

Skype is used with all the major operating systems. Apple iOS, Windows, Android, and Chrome OS. It has many features and has good voice and video quality. Skype is owned by Microsoft.

FaceTime can only be used by Apple iOS users. It cannot be used with Windows or Android. It is quick and easy to use, but only if you or those you want to call are using an Apple phone, tablet, or computer.

Google Duo and **Google Hangouts** can be enjoyed with Apple iOS, Windows, and Android devices. Your phone number is used to register an account with these apps and to link the app to your Gmail account.

Facebook Messenger and **WhatsApp.** Video calling is available from your computer or mobile phone to another device using Apple iOS, Android, or Windows. A conversation is started in Messenger where you select the video icon on the screen to begin a video call. Facebook Messenger and WhatsApp are owned by Facebook.

Zoom is known for conferencing with groups but can also be used for one-to-one video chats. It runs on Apple iOS, Windows, Android devices, and Kindle Fire. Your email address is used to register an account. An invitation or link to join the group is sent via email.

17.

Internet Safety for Children

Danger is certainly lurking as we see children under the age of two who, by watching their parents, quickly learn to swipe the face of tablets and telephones to gain access.

Supervising young children when they use a video chat app is necessary. Also important is using the parental controls and checking the privacy settings on all devices that both young and older children will have access to.

How old should a child be to use video chat unsupervised? Most video chat apps state that children must be 13 to use the app without supervision. However, unless there are parental controls and privacy settings initialized, we now know that this may not be safe, even at age 13.

Most mobile devices, phones, tablets, and e-readers have browsers that access the Internet. This gives children access to dangerous apps and unrestricted content. They also give parents the option to turn on protections for their children. Parents are responsible for setting these options.

Some working parents are experimenting with regular video chat check-ins with their children. Determining the age at which your child can use these apps depends on who the child is calling and the maturity level of that child.

Children, with the use of strong parental controls and/or monitoring, might be responsible enough to call a parent who is at work or a parent not in residence as part of a visitation plan. They may be able to safely call a grandparent, or someone else in their approved contact list.

Julie Jargon, a columnist for the Wall Street Journal, has written extensively about the impact of technology on family life. Parents and grandparents might want to explore some of her writings.

https://www.wsj.com/news/author/julie-jargon

Jargon and others have warned that the 1998 law, which has fostered the idea that 13 is the age of adulthood online is a concern for parents. She reminds us that at 13 children are more than a decade from having a fully developed prefrontal cortex, the part of the brain involved in decision-making and impulse control.

https://www.wsj.com/articles/how-13-became-the-internets-age-of-adulthood-11560850201

How then did 13 become the age tech companies recommend for access? A law called The Children's Online Privacy Act (COPPA) was passed in 1998. It was intended to protect the privacy of children and to prevent companies from collecting and sharing children's personal information. The law was passed before we had Facebook and the iPhone. Many agree that this law is not an adequate safety net for our children.

Craig Timber a national reporter covering technology for the Washington Post warns parents that sex, drugs, violence, hate speech, and talk about suicide are no more than a few clicks away from children with Internet access.

Surveys show that four out of five American preteens use some form of social media despite the online services stating officially that they prohibit users younger than 13.

Unfortunately, millions of kids when downloading apps are stating their age as older than they are, making the law ineffective and outdated. Others are creating fake accounts with older ages.

Although the law was updated in 2013 to include protections for photos, videos, geographical location, and activity tracking web cookies, the age limit was not updated.

Read Timber's informative article:

https://www.washingtonpost.com/technology/2019/06/13/sex-drugs-self-harm-where-years-child-online-protection-law-went-wrong/

Talking Tech with Children

Talking with your children about the benefits and dangers of using electronic devices is one of the most important steps that you can take to keep them safe. Start as soon as they show an interest in any electronic device, a parent's phone, tablet, or personal computer. And, be sure to start before they receive their first device.

It is just as important to be aware that children learn about technology by watching their parents. Although most parents believe they are good role models for technology use, a 2016 Commonsense study reported that parents who expressed concerns about children spending too much time with electronics, spent more time than their children. Much of that time was not work related. Remember that you are your child's most important role model.

I think back to how my own children learned to drive a car. They showed an interest from an early age and watched me closely. We talked about how to stay safe and keep others safe. They were issued learners' permits and practiced with me in the car. They studied and passed a driving test. Children's safe use of technology is just as important as learning to drive a car.

Many parents and grandparents are aware that their children and grandchildren know more about technology than they do. But children need your help in using technology wisely and safely. Just as we try to keep our children safe with good advice and reasonable limits in other aspects of their lives, we need to guide them to use technology safely and responsibly.

The Tech Talk—Two to Four Years

Curious preschoolers love to explore the Internet with parents. Spend time with them weekly. Introduce them to fun, age appropriate apps for games and education. Talk with them about what they enjoy and what they have learned. Demonstrate the importance of turning off devices properly and putting devices away with care.

Young children do not have the critical thinking skills to be online alone and could risk moving from appropriate to inappropriate sites. Keep all Internet enabled devices out of reach and protect access with passwords. Set house rules and boundaries for use from an early age. Model the importance of balance between tech time and active playtime.

The Tech Talk—Primary School Children

Primary school children 6-10 years old may be very capable using electronic devices. Many are using technology in their schools and some schools have outstanding programs to teach digital citizenship and safety online.

Parents also need to be involved in this digital education and maintain a safe place for children to talk about anything that happens online that confuses, hurts, or frightens them.

Just as you teach about the danger of some strangers, you must teach children to protect themselves by never sharing personal information online. You may want to create a poster listing the information they should never share without your permission. Include the following: their address, phone number, full name, locations, school name, photos and passwords. Put this poster near the device the child will be using or in the area where a tablet is used. Consider displaying the information on the front of your refrigerator.

For young children, parental controls need to be in place. Without strong parental controls, school age children can be exposed to online marketers or predators who encourage or even bully them into sharing personal information through surveys, contests, games, and registration forms.

All major browsers, Chrome, Firefox, Edge, and Opera include security features that can be turned on for children. Google, Yahoo, and Bing all have safe search features that you can activate in the device settings. They can block some inappropriate content but do not guarantee that they can block all cyber threats and inappropriate content.

Consider installing a kid friendly search engine. When selecting a search engine for children, you might want to consider those that don't use advertising such as Kidtopia, Kiddle or DuckDuckGo. Set age-appropriate filtering at the most restrictive levels.

Set electronic bookmarks or favorites for sites that your young children use frequently so they can go directly to the site or web page without going elsewhere. Using the settings on their devices block the use of instant messaging (IM), email, chat rooms, mobile Internet, text, video messaging, and app store purchases.

Encourage school age children to use devices in a common area in your home so you can see what sites are visited. Avoid use of devices in children's bedrooms.

Look for communication from the child's school about what they are doing with technology. Ask what the child enjoyed, what they found interesting, and if anything they saw was confusing. Have your child show you the sites they visit in school, or games that the school recommends they play.

Netsmartzkids, an Internet safety program developed by the National Center for Missing & Exploited Children, is a great resource for parents, kids, teens, and educators. It addresses online safety, cyberbullying, and online exploitation. Explore their website for videos, PowerPoint presentations, Tip Sheets, and Classroom Activities. Consider watching the videos with your children.

www.netsmartzkids.org

www.nsteens.org

The Federal Bureau of Investigation (FBI) has also developed resources to teach children about Internet safety. The FBI Safe Online Surfing (SOS) program has interactive games for learning. Playing these games and watching videos with your children is a great way to learn together about safety.

https://sos.fbi.gov/en/

Although you may set parental controls for your children, other children may not have this protection. There have been reports by children of inappropriate content being shared on the school bus. Children need to know that they can walk away from others sharing inappropriate content and they can shut down their own electronic devices if they feel uncomfortable.

If you create a comfortable atmosphere for your child to discuss technology, they are more likely to share their concerns with you and discuss what friends and school mates are doing and seeing online.

The Tech Talk—Preteens & Teens

Many preteens have mobile phones and tablets. Preteens are often interested in social media. Although 13 is the minimum age required by Skype, Facebook, and other apps, some studies have shown that 62% of 11-year-olds and 69% of 12-year-olds have Facebook profiles.

Diana Graber, in *Raising Humans in a Digital World,* discusses the many positives of digital connections for preteens and teens. She says that teens can strengthen friendships, learn to understand their friends' feelings, contribute to less peer-related loneliness, develop new friendships, and provide social support. When families use Internet related activities together, stream content, play games, and make video calls, they can improve family relationships.

If you have set house rules for device use when children are young, it will be less difficult than if you wait until the preteen or teen years. It is important to set rules about how much time can be spent using electronic devices online and to implement the rules. Continue to keep electronic devices in the open and stay in control.

Parental controls on your home broadband and on all Internet-enabled devices continue to be important to keep your preteens safe. Keeping personal information private and not sharing information about age, location, and passwords must be part of the conversation.

At this stage kids may be interested in video calls to friends as well as family. Video chat can take a dangerous turn with inappropriate relationships and conversations. Know who your child is chatting with and continue to screen video chat friends.

Introduce children to the concept of a "digital footprint." Remind them that anything that they do or say while online and during a video chat can be photographed, recorded, saved, and shared. Nothing is private.

Discuss the importance of thinking before posting or saying something online or in a text. This is part of being a good digital citizen. Treating others as you want to be treated while online is also an important discussion to have with preteens.

Don't hesitate to initiate communication about cyberbullying and sexting. Teens need to know what sexting is and understand the serious consequences of sexting. Nude, semi-nude images, and explicit texts, are all considered sexting. Federal law considers any sexually explicit image of a minor child to be pornography.

Although laws differ from state to state the government can prosecute anyone who produces, distributes or possesses child pornography. Sexting is a felony in ten states and is seen as a violation with consequences in other states. This is a talk that parents must have with their children.

Keep the communication about the Internet light and pleasant to keep your children talking. Focus on the positive. Asking what apps and sites they enjoy is a good way to stay involved in what your child is doing.

There are also several books that can be very helpful to parents, two of my favorites are: *Raising Humans in a Digital World: Helping Kids Build a Healthy Relationship with Technology* (2019) by Diana Graber, and *Screen Time Sanity: The Crazy Easy Guide to Doing Technology with Your Kids* (2018) by Kira Lewis & Michelle Myers.

Tools for Children's Safety

Privacy Settings & Parental Controls

Privacy settings and parental controls are tools that put you in control of what your child can see online. Minimize your child's risks prior to giving a phone or tablet to your child by using these tools.

There are three major types of parental controls:

1. Controls that can be set on your broadband or router that apply to all devices using that router.

2. Controls that can be set on each device your child uses like smartphones and tablets, no matter where they are used.

3. Controls that can be set on the application or platform that is being used, for example YouTube, Facebook, or Skype.

Begin by initializing the parental controls for your broadband. You can find directions for doing this online or by contacting your Internet provider.

In late 2019, Apple and Google announced efforts to improve the settings that protect children. Google extended its Family Link parental controls to teens and made it part of the latest version of the Android operating system. Apple also announced upgrades that will make it easier for parents to set time limits on iPhones and iPads and to manage children's contacts and communication.

When you combine parental controls with strong privacy settings on each device and add specific controls on the apps your child will be using, you are helping to protect the child from content that they should not experience online.

The Intel Security Company has a blog for Internet safety and keeping children safe. Explore some of their excellent articles:

https://blogs.mcafee.com/consumer/

Approving Apps

Be aware that many dangerous apps are available to children who have access to the Internet. Apps can access your device and share information about your contacts, calendar, social media accounts, location and more. Many apps request more information than they need.

Parents must know what their child is downloading and what each app does. Some apps are disguised as calculators or music managers but have other functions that permit users to see the child's location. Other apps allow children or teens to hide photos and messages that are on their devices.

Some apps promote sharing secrets with strangers and others encourage spreading rumors or bullying. Some compare kids against each other and encourage rating them. Don't be swayed if your child or teen tells you that "everyone is using the app."

Here is an example of why you should be cautious. The app TikTok (formerly named Musical.ly) now has one billion users. Launched by a Chinese-based company, users come from all over the world. In addition to the US, users come from India, Russia, Saudi Arabia, Turkey, and many other countries. Kids love this app because they can create lip-sync and other short musical videos.

The app can be dangerous when used in a public setting. It is not an app for young children. Users may be exposed to sexual content and inappropriate language. There are reports of online predators using this app. If older children use the app be sure it is set to private rather than public mode. Consider using the apps new Family Safety mode to easily monitor connections and content when the app is used.

Do some research and remove all apps that you haven't approved and be sure settings are private on those that are used. There are many articles online and websites that evaluate apps.

You might want to learn more about apps by exploring Common Sense Media and Internet Matters:

https://www.commonsensemedia.org/app-reviews

https://www.internetmatters.org/resources/apps-guide/

Managing Contacts

Parents must discuss with children and teens the importance of never accepting chat requests from anyone they do not know. Accepting a call from someone not in the contact list can be dangerous for both adults and children. Predators often mask as friends or someone who knows a family member.

Review your contact list and any lists that your child will be using. Delete contacts that you do not want to communicate with or any that have been randomly added by other apps or websites.

Teach children to immediately close the video chat if they receive a call from a stranger or if someone who is calling does or says inappropriate things. That is also the best action if the child is bullied via video chat. Video bulling does occur. Instruct children to block bullies and tell you about it.

Monitoring Tools for Parents

Good communication with your children is one of the best ways to keep them safe. Everyone agrees that monitoring the child's use of their devices is important. Unfortunately, it's not always easy for parents to see and know what a child is doing, especially when they are using several different devices. Parental control services can help. These are tools for monitoring device and app usage.

There are third party products that allow parents to set custom profiles for each child. You can restrict specific websites and apps as well as limit time spent on an app or on the device. Read more on the Internet about Qustodio, Net Nanny, and others. Check the latest reviews for these products.

Safety & Skype

Skype's websites and software are not intended for or designed to attract users under the age of 13. Skype encourages parents to be involved in the online activities of their children to make sure that no information is collected from a child without parental permission.

Skype has security measures in place to help protect children who have parental permission to use Skype from being contacted by strangers. Their security measures are based on the date of birth provided by the user when creating a profile. It is very important for parents to enter the correct information, while leaving personal information out of the profile pages, so others cannot see this information.

You can hide children from random search results by turning off "Appear in search results."

You can find the Skype safety information here:

https://support.skype.com/en/faq/FA10548/what-security-measures-do-you-have-in-place-to-help-protect-children-on-skype

Safety & FaceTime

Thirteen is also the minimum age FaceTime recommends for children's use without a parent present. They recommend that parents use *Settings* to turn off the option to use FaceTime and to turn it on when a parent is present. For older children who know how to get to the settings you may want to consider a password to protect the device. The FaceTime password should be different than the device or Apple password.

You can find helpful information about Parental Controls on your child's iPhone here:

https://www.cnet.com/how-to/parental-controls-you-can-use-right-now-on-your-kids-iphone/

Many of the large tech companies are beginning to develop better systems to help keep children safe while online. After choosing a video chat app check the parental controls and settings that are available to you.

18.

Safety for Adults Online

In addition to safety concerns for children, adults must take steps to stay safe and protect their privacy. Grandparents beware as scammers specifically target older adults. Using this technology safely will enhance your enjoyment of the video call applications.

Passwords

Start by creating a strong password for your video chat app and all other online sites that you create. A strong password is one that will not be easily broken. It may also prevent others from hacking or gaining access to the information on your computer.

If you think using the word "password" for your password or the numerical sequence 1-2-3-4-5 is safe, think again. These passwords are among the most used and easy to break passwords.

Many safety experts suggest using a three-word phrase and modifying it to include letters with mixed cases, symbols and numbers. For example, instead of "over ten million," substitute numbers and symbols and vary the case: oVer10mi$lioN.

With Skype you will create your unique username and a password. FaceTime requires you to use your Apple ID and email address, and with Google Duo you will need a Google+ account with your username and password or your telephone number.

Using a password manager can assist in keeping you safe and organized. Password managers are programs that store your log-in information (usernames and passwords) online. They can also assist in generating and retrieving complex passwords.

The password manager lists all the websites that you use and automatically logs you in when you select the website that you want to visit.

Examples of password managers include Dashlane, LastPass, Keeper, and Sticky. Most of these managers have free downloads for you to try. You can read reviews of these managers online. Be cautious that you are reading a review and not an advertisement.

Protect Personal Information

Opt out of entering your birthdate, location or telephone number into the profiles of social media sites. This information may be available to the public. Never provide personal information to someone who calls you on the telephone. Don't give your full name, address, credit card or bank information to anyone you don't know personally.

Protect Your computer

Protect your computer with an antivirus program and a firewall. A firewall protects your computer from unauthorized access to or from your computer. Your router can act as a firewall if it is secured with a password. Secure your Wi-Fi router with a strong password so others will not have access to your computer.

Be on guard when you are using your computer or telephone, especially for email. Never open attachments or click on links in email from someone that you don't know. Something as simple as a cartoon or poem can carry viruses into your device. Even if you receive an email from a person you recognize, if there is a link with no message do not click on that link. Some of these links come from computers that have been hacked.

Summary

New forms of communication are continually being developed and changing. When my grandparents immigrated to this country it took weeks to exchange letters with family members in another country. Many who relocated never saw or talked to their family members again.

Today we can see and talk with family and friends around the world in seconds using video chat. You may not be able to be physically present with a child or grandchild, but we now know that we can develop a close bond using this wonderful technology.

Let me assure you that video chat apps are easy to use and a lot of fun. The small amount of effort it takes to get set up will bring you great rewards. Within a short time, you will feel like an expert and much prefer video chat to telephone calls.

It doesn't take a lot of preparation. Most likely you already have a device you can use and the app that you need for your personal computer, tablet or phone. It takes only seconds to connect. Get some help from a family member or friend, but don't delay in trying this amazing technology.

Although this book presents many suggestions for interactive activities, there are times when my grandchildren have their own plan. Some of the best calls happen spontaneously with no plan at all. These are fun calls when I say hello and then just sit back, relax, and chat with my grandchildren and their parents. Envision watching a child you love eager to show and tell you about their latest experience or interest.

Interacting with a child using the suggestions in this book can enhance both your experience and that of the child. Big smiles and lots of enthusiasm often come when I have planned an activity or share with the children one of their favorite puppets or books.

In the preschool years, my grandchildren enjoyed playing with a small dump truck when they visited my home. When we were apart, moving that truck across the web cam, so they could see it on the screen, instantly got their attention. There were peals of laughter when I placed small toys like a rubber duck or a small soft monkey in the back of the truck and dump it out. As they have grown older, they still occasionally ask to see those toys. Although they certainly have grown out of the toys, they love finding them in my storage chest when they come to visit.

Nothing is too silly for a child to enjoy, so when you video chat let your imagination soar and don't be afraid to bring out your own inner child.

While the technology of video call appears safe on the surface, anytime a child accesses the Internet, they need you to keep them safe. While updating this book I have become aware that having open and regular conversations about Internet safety with children is necessary to keep them safe. Good communication along with the use of parental controls on the devices that children will use is as important as holding a child's hand crossing the street or teaching your teen to drive safely.

If you are a grandparent reading this book, share this information with your adult children. Parents will be setting the parental controls and doing most of the communicating about safety.

Video chat will help you stay connected to family that you are separated from. It will assist you in building a special relationship and a close bond with the children you love. Don't miss out on the fun of video chat.

Technical Terms You Will Want to Know

The following terms will help you understand the basics of computing and video calling. Refer to this glossary if you come across a term that you don't already know.

APPLICATION OR APP

A software program that helps you perform a task. App is an abbreviation for application. There are apps for both desktop use and for mobile devices such as tablets and phones. Skype, FaceTime, Facebook, YouTube, Uber and Google Maps are examples of apps.

BOOKMARK

A bookmark or electronic bookmark is a way to save web page addresses. In some web browsers, bookmarks are called Favorites.

BROADBAND

The term broadband is short for broadband Internet access and refers to a high-speed data transmission. The most common types of Internet broadband connections are cable, DSL, wireless, satellite, and fiber optics.

BROWSER

An Internet or web browser is a program that allows you to go to websites or webpages. Apple Safari, Opera, Chrome, Mozilla Firefox, Internet Explorer, and Netscape Communicator are all web browsers. A browser will be installed on any computer or smartphone that you purchase. You can also download any others you choose for free.

CAPTCHA

A verification process that requires users to enter distorted letters into a form or to solve a puzzle. CAPTCHA stands for Completely Automated Public Turing test. It is used to tell Computer Bots (robots) and Humans apart. It is a security measure that helps to keep the Internet spam free.

COMPUTER HARDWARE

Refers to all physical parts of a computer, the processor, monitor, keyboard, and mouse. Hardware also includes the interior components of a computer.

COMPUTER SOFTWARE

Includes all the programed instructions that tell the computer what to do. This includes the programs and applications. Examples include Microsoft Office, browsers such as Chrome, and applications like Pandora and Skype.

CONTACT

People that you know and want to communicate with.

CYBER

A prefix meaning related to computer, computer network or virtual reality. Used in the formation of compound words, cyberspace, cyberbullying.

CYBERBULLYING

The use of technology to harass, threaten, embarrass, or target another person.

DEVICE

A piece of equipment or component designed to serve a specific purpose. In technology and computer systems it often refers to equipment that attaches to or works with the computer. Examples include the keyboard, mouse, or printer. Mobile devices include smartphones, tablets, and laptop computers.

DIGITAL CITIZENSHIP

The appropriate use of digital technology. Transferring the characteristics of traditional citizenship, responsibility, honesty, respect for diversity, and compassion for others, to online communities.

DIGITAL FOOTPRINT

The information about a person that exists on the Internet as a result of that person's online activity.

DOWNLOAD

To download something from the web means to copy it from a website to your computer. Many things can be downloaded: data, books, movies, and software applications.

ENCRYPTION

The process of converting information or data into code to prevent unauthorized access.

FILTER

To set conditions so only certain information is displayed when visiting the web. It can block unwanted content such as pornography and protect the device from malware. Spam filters can help prevent unwanted email from reaching your inbox. Parental controls filter content.

HARDWARE

The physical parts of a computer and related devices.

HEADSET

A device with a microphone that is worn on your head and leaves your hands free. There are headsets that need to be plugged into the computer and wireless headsets.

HYPERLINK

A link to a file or document that can be a graphic, icon, or text which the reader can follow with a click or tap to access another file or object.

ICON

An icon is a symbol that represents the application (or part of the application) that you want to use.

INTERNET

The Internet is an enormous networking infrastructure. It connects millions of computers together globally so any computer can communicate with any other computer if both are connected to the Internet.

MENU

Sometimes called a drop-down list or drop-down menu, the menu is a list of options or choices. The menu provides access to functions such as opening and closing files and editing text and closing programs. Menus are accessed by placing a mouse or a finger on the menu bar

MODEM

A hardware component that allows the computer to connect to the Internet.

OPERATING SYSTEM

A system of software that runs the computer. It manages the computer's processes and memory. Microsoft Windows and Apple iOS are examples of operating systems.

PARENTAL CONTROLS

Software installed on computers and mobile devices that lets parents set controls for children's computer use.

PLATFORM

The basic hardware and software upon which software applications can be run. Operating systems like Windows, Android, and iOS are examples of platforms.

PRIVACY SETTINGS

Settings on a phone or computer that help protect against privacy invasion. Settings allow users to grant or block information sharing.

PASSWORD

A string of characters or a phrase that allows or protects access to a computer system, device, or service.

ROUTER

A router is Internet hardware that transfers Internet messages. It helps provide a good Internet connection and speedy Wi-Fi.

SEARCH ENGINE

Programs that search the Internet for specified keywords and return a list of the places where the keywords are found. A search engine is a program found in all Internet browsers that enables users to find information on the World Wide Web. Google and Yahoo are the most popular search engines. Examples of search engines for kids are Kidtopia, Kiddle and DuckDuckGo.

SEXTING

Digitally sending or sharing of sexually explicit images or texts.

SOFTWARE

Includes all the computer codes, programs, and instructions that tell a computer what to do.

USB PORT

Short for Universal Serial Bus, this is where an electronic device, such as a keyboard, mouse, webcam, or headset, is connected to your computer. It supplies the power to the device.

VIDEO

Video relates to visual images. It originally pertained to television images. Video technology includes video tape and video clips for computers. In a video call, a live picture of the person making the call as well as the person receiving the call is transmitted, both can see each other.

VIDEO CHAT

Video chat, video call, and video conference all describe an audio as well as visual communication between two people using an Internet connection and a software application like Skype or FaceTime.

VIRTUAL VISITATION

Virtual visitation is a form of child visitation that requires the use of technology. Sometimes called electronic communication or Internet communication, it can include video call, email, instant messaging, social networks, or other forms of communication posted on the Internet.

WEBCAM

The term webcam is a combination of two words, web representing the World Wide Web and cam for video camera. A webcam is a camera that is installed on a computer, tablet, or phone. An external camera can be attached to the computer monitor or sit on a desk.

WEBSITE

A website is a page or group of interconnected pages that are found on the Internet.

WI-FI

A technology that allows for the transfer of information wirelessly using radio waves. Wi-Fi is a trademark of the Wi-Fi Alliance and is used as part of brand names for products.

WORLD WIDE WEB

The World Wide Web or simply the Web is a way of accessing information over the Internet. The web utilizes browsers to access information on web pages as well as to access graphics, sounds, and videos.

133

YOUTUBE

YouTube is a website and video hosting platform. It has evolved from a simple video input and sharing website to the second largest search engine after Google. YouTube was purchased by Google in 2006. The platform is used by both amateurs and professionals.

Acknowledgements

A special thank you to the friends and family who have enthusiastically shared their stories about the fun they have with video chat. A huge thank you to the dear friends who generously gave their time to read my manuscript and who provided support, and encouragement as well as insightful and constructive advice. I especially want to thank Ardel Nelson, Mary Ann Needham, Marcia Lisser, and Pat Wheeler.

I also wish to thank my daughter Lynn Grimes and son Chris Tibbles who shared their perspective as parents and utilized this technology to keep our family close.

It was a pleasure to work with Travis Miles who designed my book cover and with Kimberly Hitchens and the staff at Booknook.biz.

If you found my book helpful, I would be very grateful if you would consider writing a review. Reviews can play a big part in helping other parents and grandparents to discover the joy of video chat.

Resources

AARP & Microsoft. (2012). *Connecting generations report of the AARP & Microsoft survey and focus groups findings,* from: https://assets.aarp.org/rgcenter/general/Connecting-Generations.pdf

American Academy of Pediatrics. (2016). *Policy statement: Media & young Minds:* from: https://pediatrics.aappublications.org/content/138/5/e20162591

Allyn, P. (2009). *What to read when.* New York: Penguin.

Altman, T. (Ed). (2019) *American Academy of Pediatrics. Caring for your baby and young child: birth to 5 years.* New York. Bantam Books.

Common Sense Media. (2016). *The Commonsense census: Plugged-in parents of tweens and teens,* from: https://www.commonsensemedia.org/sites/default/files/uploads/research/common-sense-parent-census_executivesummary_for-web.pdf

Cytrynbaum, P. (2013) College students tell parents how to communicate with them, from: https://www.psychologytoday.com/us/blog/because-im-the-mom/201306/college-students-tell-parents-how-communicate-them

Einon, D. (2004). *How children learn through play.* Hauppauge, N. Y.: Barron's.

Favaro, P. (2009). *Smart parenting during and after divorce.* New York: McGraw Hill.

Graber D. (2019). *Raising humans in a digital world: Helping kids build a healthy relationship with technology.* New York: Harper Collins.

Hayes, L. & Cohen, D. (2010). *The Yale child study center guide to understanding your child.* Boston: Little Brown.

Hofer, B. & Moore A. (2013) *The iConnected parent: Staying close to your kids in college (and beyond) while letting them grow up.* New York: Atria.

Jargon, J. November 28, 2019. *How 13 became the Internet's age for adulthood,* from: https://www.wsj.com/articles/how-13-became-the-internets-age-of-adulthood-11560850201

Leach, P. *The essential first year.* (2010). New York: Dorling Kindersley.

Lewis, K. & Myers, M. (2018). *Screen time sanity: The crazy easy guide to doing technology with your kids.* Lumos Press.

Shaywitz, S. & Shaywitz, B. (August 25, 2016). *Dyslexia: Cracking the code,* from: https://www.cbsnews.com/video/dyslexia-cracking-the-code/

Stamm, J. (2008). *Bright from the Start: The simple, science backed way to nurture your child's developing mind from birth to age 3.* New York, Penguin Group.

Timberg, C. June 13, 2019. *Sex, drugs, and self-harm: Where 20 years of child online protection law went wrong,* from: https://www.washingtonpost.com/technology/2019/06/13/sex-drugs-self-harm-where-years-child-online-protection-law-went-wrong/

HELPFUL WEBSITES

www.babycenter.com

www.cdc.gov/ncbddd/childdevelopment

www.scholastic.com

www.pbs.org/parents

https://www.aap.org/en-us/about-the-aap/aap-press-room/news-features-and-safety-tips/Pages/Children-and-Media-Tips.aspx

Communicating with Children and Teens

http://understandingteenagers.com.au/blog/5-mistakes-adults-make-communicating-with-teenagers/

https://www.psychologytoday.com/blog/hope-relationships/201404/9-tips-communicating-your-teenage-son

http://www.cnn.com/2014/02/19/living/talking-to-teens-communication-parents

Divorced Parents

www.raisingchildren.net.au

www.parents.com

Dyslexia

https://dyslexia.yale.edu/

http://www.mayoclinic.org/diseases-conditions/dyslexia/basics/definition/con-20021904

Internet Safety

https://www.wsj.com/news/author/julie-jargon

https://www.washingtonpost.com/technology/2019/06/13/sex-drugs-self-harm-where-years-child-online-protection-law-went-wrong/

https://www.commonsensemedia.org/app-reviews

https://www.winknews.com/2019/02/25/apps-that-could-put-your-kids-in-danger/

https://www.connectsafely.org/

https://www.tigermobiles.com/blog/how-to-protect-your-children-on-their-smartphone/

https://Internetsafety101.org/agebasedguidlines

https://www.fbi.gov/fbi-kids

https://sos.fbi.gov/

https://blogs.mcafee.com/consumer/

Technical Support

https://support.skype.com/en/faq/FA34542/how-do-i-set-up-and-use-skype-translator

https://www.cnet.com/how-to/parental-controls-you-can-use-right-now-on-your-kids-iphone/

https://www.commonsensemedia.org/parent-concerns

https://www.Internetmatters.org/parental-controls/

https://healthychildren.org/english/media/pages/default.aspx#home

https://www.missingkids.org/NetSmart

Lillian Tibbles, PhD, is an author and retired psychiatric/mental health nurse practitioner and family therapist. She received both a master's degree and PhD from the University of Connecticut. As a graduate student in the early '80s, she used a mainframe computer, at the university, to analyze data and write her dissertation. Thus, began her interest in the benefits of technology. She has published articles about the use of computers for patient education and three books about video call with children. Her three grandchildren living far away inspired her interest in video chat.

Visit her website and blog

www.videocallwithkids.com

Index

www.ingramcontent.com/pod-product-compliance
Lightning Source LLC
Chambersburg PA
CBHW071200050326
40689CB00011B/2197